Stead, W. Edward.
Management for a small planet : strategic decision making and the environment / W. Edward Stead, Jean Garner Stead. -- Newberry Park, Calif. : Sage Publications, c1992.
xii, 212 p. : ill. ; 24 cm.
Includes bibliographical references (p. 192-201) and indexes.
ISBN 0-8039-4635-X (pbk.)
ISBN 0-8039-4634-1

1. Economic development--Environmental aspects. 2. Natural resources--Management. 3. Strategic planning. 4. Industrial management--Environmental aspects. I. Stead, Jean Garner. II. Title.

Management for a Small Planet

To our parents, who motivate us from the past;
To the oneness of our relationship, which motivates us in the present;
To Garner Lee and Valerie, who motivate us for the future.
May the past, present, and future generations of the Earth survive eternity.

Management for a Small Planet

STRATEGIC DECISION MAKING AND THE ENVIRONMENT

W. Edward Stead
Jean Garner Stead

SAGE PUBLICATIONS
International Educational and Professional Publisher
Newbury Park London New Delhi

For information address:

SAGE Publications, Inc.
2455 Teller Road
Newbury Park, California 91320

SAGE Publications Ltd.
6 Bonhill Street
London EC2A 4PU
United Kingdom

SAGE Publications India Pvt. Ltd.
M-32 Market
Greater Kailash I
New Delhi 110 048 India

Printed in the United States of America

Library of Congress Cataloging-in-Publication Data

Stead, W. Edward.
Management for a small planet: strategic decision making and the environment / W. Edward Stead, Jean Garner Stead.
p. cm.
Includes bibliographical references and index.
ISBN 0-8039-4634-1.—ISBN 0-8039-4635-X (pbk.)
1. Economic development—Environmental aspects. 2. Natural resources—Management. 3. Strategic planning. 4. Industrial mangement—Environmental aspects. I. Stead, Jean Garner. II. Title.
HD75.6.S74 1992
333.7—dc20 92-2644

92 93 94 95 10 9 8 7 6 5 4 3

Sage Production Editor: Chiara C. Huddleston

Printed on recycled paper 

Contents

Preface

As humankind rapidly approaches the third millennium, it becomes more apparent that society must reconcile economic activity with the limits of the small planet Earth. Strategic decision makers in business organizations choose what to produce, how to produce it, how to package it, and so on; they must begin making these choices within the context of an economic framework that stresses the long-term survival of the human species. Indeed, this already seems to be happening in many corners of industry as well as in the public sector. It is heartening to see that consumers, investors, business organizations, and governments are all becoming aware of ecological issues.

This book serves as a guide for strategic managers making critical economic decisions in the coming decades, decisions that will have the potential to affect the delicate balance of the ecosystem. Although business managers are often portrayed as bad guys where environmental protection is concerned, we have a deep respect for the integrity of these individuals. We interact with them regularly in our educational and consulting activities and find that most are good people who try to do the right things. We believe that business managers can and will change the values and approaches they use in making strategic decisions, if they can be educated as to why such changes are necessary and how they can be made.

If humankind is to evolve toward a more ecologically safe economic system, it must recognize that protecting the Earth is an issue that transcends traditional left-right politics. Environmental protection is neither the exclusive bailiwick of the political left, nor the nonissue, as it is so often portrayed, of the political right. We believe that continuing the left versus right debate about the natural environment will contribute little to finding the necessary solutions. We all live on this planet together; thus we all have a stake in its continued viability. We must work together to solve its problems.

The odyssey of this book began in 1980 at Louisiana State University in Baton Rouge, where the seeds were planted by two scholars: Herman E. Daly, Professor of Economics at LSU; and Edmund R. Gray, Professor and Chairperson of the Management Department at LSU. Both were heavily involved in early efforts to define more clearly the role of business within the greater society in which it exists. We would like to express our deepest gratitude to these gentlemen. They provided us with the foundation of knowledge we needed to begin our journey and encouraged us to bring our ideas to fruition; they have been true friends throughout our relationship with them. Neither of these gentlemen is at LSU any longer. Dr. Daly is an environmental economist with the World Bank in Washington, DC, and Dr. Gray is a professor in the Management Department at Loyola Marymount University in Los Angeles.

About the time we became acquainted with these gentlemen, our daughter was born. So while these scholars were planting the academic seeds of this book, Garner Lee was providing us with the emotional motivation we needed to commit ourselves to a sustainable economic future. She, too, was a teacher to us in the past decade. She taught us that the basic needs and hopes of humankind are founded on the desire to continue as a species. She taught us that the preservation of the Earth is the way to ensure this continuity for posterity. She taught us that we are only a small link in the chain of human existence, and that it is our responsibility to keep the chain strong for generations to come. Through her we realized that we borrow this planet from our children. She taught us all of this through her unconditional love; her simple, insightful questions and observations; and her burning desire from the beginning to have a family and a career of her own in a world of beauty and safety. To her goes our deepest gratitude for all the knowledge and spiritual meaning she has bestowed on us.

The final seed for this book was planted in the mountains of Northeast Tennessee where we have resided for the past 10 years. Our home is a true ecological treasure with its spectacular mountain ranges; beautiful rivers, streams, and lakes; wide variety of life; and rich history. Unfortunately, our home also has serious environmental problems: Superfund sites, polluted waterways, high-level nuclear wastes, overflowing landfills, severe acid rain, and some of the nation's worst air pollution. Most of these problems are rooted in the business activities of the region. All one need do is view our mountains on a misty morning or watch a creek cascade down a rocky hillside to realize that we must find a sustainable balance between business activity and the Earth.

We would like to thank the many people who assisted us, in one way or another, in the preparation of this book. Thanks to Glen Riecken, Chairperson of East Tennessee State University's Management and Marketing Department, and to Allan Spritzer, Dean of East Tennessee State University's College of Business. Together they provided an academic environment that encouraged us to pursue our research even though it did not always follow a traditional business vein. We especially thank them for (a) allowing us to offer our experimental course on management and the natural environment, which provided us with a laboratory to test our ideas and approaches on the ideal audience—students of business; and (b) supporting Ed's noninstructional assignment in the spring of 1991 so that this manuscript could be completed.

We again thank Ed Gray of Loyola Marymount University, John Kilpatrick of Idaho State University, Alonzo Smith of Mankato State University, and Kathleen Dechant of the University of Connecticut, who helped us by reviewing the original manuscript. Thanks also to Dan Worrell of Appalachian State University for reviewing Chapter 8 and for always being willing to discuss the book with us. Special thanks go to Amanda Moss for her diligent, timely, and professional editorial help, to Valerie Brown for her excellent graphic artwork, and to Rick Watson for his help in proofing the galleys. The comments, suggestions, and contributions of these individuals have been invaluable to the final product.

We would also like to thank our graduate students, Donna Hawley, Diana Thompson, Scott Stout, Beth Fennell, and Amanda Moss (again) who put in countless hours, contributed many good ideas, and endured us with incredible patience for the past three years while we collected our information and thoughts. Thanks as well to Rob Lytle, a counselor in ETSU's Small Business Development Center, and Mark Blizzard, improvements manager of Morrison Molded Fiber Glass Company, who gave us dozens of useful references. Many others also supported our efforts, and we thank each and every one of them.

PART ONE

Introduction to a Small Planet

What is a small planet? Of what concern is this concept to strategic decision makers in today's business organizations? What problems occur as the planet gets smaller and smaller? In this section we attempt to answer these questions and to introduce the dimensions and problems of a small planet. We discuss the fundamental reasons why economic activity is currently at odds with ecological sustainability and examine the role of the strategic manager in light of this. We then examine the current environmental issues more fully, focusing on their causes and their potentially devastating outcomes.

Chapter 1

It's Time for a Change

An old pygmy myth goes something like this. Every morning a little boy wakes up to hear what is surely the most beautiful song on Earth coming from the world's most beautiful bird. The little boy cannot resist the temptation to own the bird, and so he sets a trap, captures it, and brings it home to sing just for him. His father, however, does not approve of feeding the bird just for the benefit of its song. That night, after the little boy is asleep, the father takes the bird into the forest and kills it. But when the bird dies, the father also drops dead on the same spot: With the bird goes the song, and with the song goes the man (Campbell, 1988).

What message does this myth hold for humankind today? Just as the boy uses his superior brain and technology to control the bird for his own purposes, humankind uses those same tools to control nature for its own ends. Just as the father makes an economic decision to destroy the bird and its beautiful song, humankind consistently destroys the natural beauty and resources of the Earth for short-term economic benefits. And just as the death of the father follows the death of the bird, humankind risks its own survival by destroying the natural environment that supports it.

Humankind has reached a point in its history when it needs to reassess where it is going and how it will get there. For the past 300 years, humans have built their hopes and dreams on the concept of unlimited economic growth. The desire for economic growth has been raised to mythic proportions that rival any religion in human history. Joseph Campbell (1988) proposes that you can tell which institution a society considers most important by the relative height of its buildings. In medieval times, the churches were the tallest buildings. During the Renaissance and the Reformation, the tallest buildings were the seats of government. Today, the tallest buildings are the centers of economic activity. Personal and societal welfare are measured almost solely on the amount of growth experienced in economic activities. More production and consumption are good. Less production and consumption are bad. It is as simple as that.

Yet, as society continues at breakneck speed to produce-consume, produce-consume, produce-consume, it does so with the knowledge that eventually the very resources that support life on this planet will be exhausted. If humans continue to foul the air and water, degrade the land, and exploit the natural beauty, the human species is in danger of disappearing. It will kill its bird, it will kill its song, and it will kill itself. Father Thomas Berry (1988) says this:

> The mythic drive [for economic growth] continues to control our world even though much is known about the Earth, its limited resources, the interdependence of life systems, the delicate balance of the ecosystems, including the consequences of disturbing atmospheric conditions, of contaminating the air, soil, waterways, and seas. The drive continues despite the limited quantities of fossil fuels in the Earth and the inherent danger of chemicals discharged into natural surroundings. Although all of this has been known for generations, neither the study nor commercial-industrial practice of economics has shown any capacity to break free from the mythic commitment to progress, or any awareness that we are in reality creating wasteworld rather than wonderworld. (p. 76)

Now is the time to break free from the mythic drive for economic growth. Humans need a new economic myth based on the society of the planet (Campbell, 1988). The environmental crisis is rapidly reaching epic proportions. Recent environmental issues include: the depletion of the upper ozone layer, the devastation of lakes and mountaintops by acid rain, the potential for rising global temperatures, the death and destruction caused by toxic spills and dumps, the massive deforestation of the world's rain forests for commercial purposes, and the harm caused by numerous oil spills. These problems make it clear that strategic decision makers in business organizations need to reorient their choices by accounting for the limits of the ecosystem. Managers who make strategic decisions concerning what products to produce, how to produce them, how to sell them, and so on, are in need of new approaches and frameworks that incorporate assumptions and values concordant with the limits of human survival on the planet.

Purpose of the Book

This book aims to prepare managers to make strategic decisions that are both economically successful and sensitive to the Earth's natural environment. More specifically, the book is designed to (a) educate managers about current national and global environmental issues, especially as they relate to economic activity; (b) provide managers with an awareness of the social, scientific, psychological, and economic concepts related to making environmentally sensitive strategic decisions; and (c) provide managers with a new strategic decision-making framework that will aid them in achieving long-term economic success within the limits of the ecosystem.

A Basic Model of Business and the Ecosystem

What role do the strategic decisions made by individuals in business organizations play in protecting or destroying the ecosystem? This question can best be addressed by realizing that the Earth is a living system; as such, it can survive only by achieving a sustainable balance within its various subsystems. Achieving a sustainable balance means maintaining levels of resource use, industrial activity, agriculture, population growth, and so on, that can be sustained for generations to come.

The most basic subsystems on Earth are composed of the individual organisms that inhabit it, and, of course, the most dominant of the planet's individual organisms is the human. Because of this dominance, the decisions made by humans are major forces influencing the ultimate state of the planet. Ornstein and Ehrlich (1990) point out that the ability of humans to make correct choices concerning their interaction with the planet depends on the accuracy of the mental processes used to make those choices. What people perceive and how they perceive it determines how they react to it. For example, if a person perceives time in terms of a human life span, then 100 years seems to be a long time. Using such a time horizon means that 5- or 10-year periods are considered long-term planning. What if time is perceived in terms of the age of the Earth though? In that case, a 100-year life span amounts to only about 1/45,000,000 of the total 4.5 billion years survived by the Earth thus far. Such a perception makes 5- or 10-year periods anything but long-term. Obviously, these widely varying perceptions of the same 100 years can lead individuals to make vastly different decisions about how they use the Earth's resources.

Humans make choices in a variety of contexts, and normally those choices are made in some collective sense. Decisions are made in the context of business organizations, educational institutions, governmental agencies, and religious denominations, to name but a few. As Etzioni (1988) points out, there is often divergence and conflict among these collectives, leading to tension within the individual members because of their varying commitments, desires, and values. In the economic realm, individuals are members of organizations that produce goods and services, as well as part of the collective of consumers who purchase and use these goods and services, or who invest in the financial performance potential of these organizations. Decisions are made in both of these contexts even though each may require different perceptions, assumptions, values, and ethics.

Of course, these collectives do not exist in isolation. Together, production and consumption make up what is referred to as the economy, the subsystem that encompasses all global business activities. This economic subsystem is normally depicted as a simple circular flow between production and consumption. According to neoclassical economics, costs and benefits of economic activities can be confined to this circular-flow model, for all practical purposes dismissing factors outside the model as simply insignificant externalities.

This may have been acceptable earlier in human history, but current circumstances, such as rapid population growth and environmental problems resulting from global economic activity, dictate that humankind can no longer ignore these factors. Humans simply cannot afford to dismiss the limits of the planet or the greater community and society in which economic activity takes place. Fritjof Capra (1983) states:

> Economists generally fail to recognize that the economy is merely one aspect of a whole ecological and social fabric; a living system composed of human beings in continual interaction with one another and with their natural resources, most of which are, in turn, living organisms. (p. 188)

It seems only logical to acknowledge that global economic activity must function within the natural and social boundaries of the planet. It certainly has no place else to function. The Earth is the ultimate source of economic capital because it is the only source of those natural resources that are converted to goods and services in the economic subsystem. As Herman E. Daly (1977) and others have pointed out repeatedly, the circular flow of economic activity can only be sustained over the long run if business recognizes that economic activity must function within the limits of Earth. The economic decisions made by individuals and organizations occur socially in the context of norms, values, emotions, and morals emitted by the larger society. Yet Etzioni (1988) contends that these social factors are ignored in economic theory.

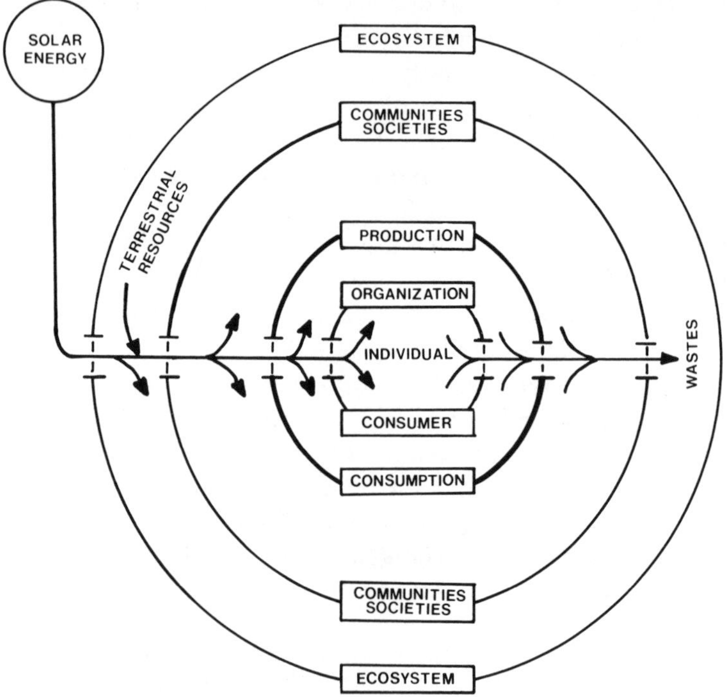

Figure 1.1. A Basic Model of Business and the Ecosystem.

In sum (as depicted in Figure 1.1), individual organisms form the most elementary subsystems of the planet, and humans are the most dominant single species. Humans are a collective species who participate in economic activities by making decisions as consumers, members of business organizations, or, quite often, both. These decisions are based on individual perceptions of reality and involve the application of values, beliefs, assumptions, and ethics. Taken as a whole, these business organizations and consumer patterns comprise the circular-flow economic subsystem of production and consumption. However, this economic subsystem is earthbound, and thus can only function within the greater society and ecosystem. All of which point to the fact that individual decision makers apply their values to the economic decisions they make, both as members of business organizations and as consumers of goods and services. Collectively, then, human values guide the production-consumption cycle. Thus if the human species desires to maintain a sustainable balance of the Earth's subsystems over the long run, economic values that are consistent with the limits of the Earth need to be adopted.

The Earth Is a Small Planet

Humans tend to perceive the Earth as a large, expansive space with unlimited resources that can support humankind's activities regardless of the scale and nature of those activities. Nothing could be further from the truth. The planet is small, and its capacity to support successive generations of humans is both limited and threatened. Let's examine why the Earth is a small planet and getting smaller.

Unprecedented Population Growth in the Industrial Age

On the outer edges of a spinning cluster of stars and other heavenly bodies called the Milky Way galaxy lies a blue-green planet known as the Earth. The Earth has evolved from a hot, gaseous ball to a planet rich with the ingredients of life—breathable air, fresh water, abundant minerals, and so on—in approximately 4.5 billion years. Life began on Earth as single-celled algae (prokaryotes) some 3.8 billion years ago; today there are between 4 million and 30 million species living on the planet, of which only 1.4 million have been formally classified. The evolutionary processes of the Earth have resulted in an incredible ecological balance between plant life, animal life, and the organic materials that support both (Tobias, 1990; Wilson, 1989). For example, an atmosphere that contains 21% oxygen has evolved. If this percentage were slightly lower, larger species (such as humans) would not have enough oxygen to survive. If this percentage were slightly higher, the toxic effects of the gas would also threaten human survival (Lovelock, 1990).

For the past 100,000 years, the Earth has been inhabited by a species known as Homo sapiens—humankind. The uniqueness of this species can be recognized in its name. The word *sapiens* comes from the Latin verb *sapere,* which means to be wise. Thus Homo sapiens is the intelligent species, "the one with the brains" as one popular TV commercial puts it. The human brain is so powerful that it can design and build machines that are able to store and process millions of times the amount of information the brain itself could handle. Frederick Taylor saw the perfect worker as an extension of his machine; to the contrary, humankind's machines are extensions of itself.

Before 1750 people employed their machines in very limited ways, using wheels for wagons and grain mills, for example. Most of the population was engaged in agriculture, a 10,000-year-old activity, and most people spent their time simply trying to survive. Life was hard and tenuous, and thus population growth was slow. There were 250 million people on Earth when Christ was born, and only 500 million people on Earth in 1650—it took more than a millennium and a half for the population to double (Ehrlich & Ehrlich, 1990). Then came the industrial revolution with its powerful fossil fuel energy sources, mass production techniques, and modern transportation and communication systems. In only 250 years humankind moved away from older forms of society whose primary activities were hunting, raising livestock, planting, and gathering, to the modern industrial societies of today.

During that period, survival became much easier and more secure. Modern farming techniques make it possible to raise more food than humans can consume. High-speed transportation and communications make it possible to speak with anyone in the world in a matter of seconds and to carry on a face-to-face conversation with them in a matter of hours. Modern medicine has transformed deadly illnesses of the past century into minor irritations today. The result being that the human species' ability to survive has greatly improved, resulting in an unprecedented growth in the number of Homo sapiens. The population, which had previously taken some 1,650 years to double, doubled again to 1 billion by 1850. From 1850 to 1987, the population multiplied fivefold to 5 billion, and the United Nations now estimates that this figure will reach between 10 and 14 billion by the year 2025.

The Earth isn't getting any bigger. This beautiful blue marble is still only 25,000 miles in circumference, three-quarters water, and much of the rest uninhabitable mountain and desert land. The Earth's natural resources are being depleted and wastes are being generated at rates unheard-of in human history. At current rates of consumption, the world's oil reserves will be depleted in 35 years, copper reserves will be depleted in 41 years, and nickel reserves will be depleted in 66 years; when the world's population reaches 10 billion, these figures are predicted to drop to 3 years, 4 years, and 7 years, respectively (Frosch & Gallopoulos, 1989). Wastes generated from product packaging increased 200% in the past 30 years; this is a major reason why more than half the cities in the United States have already exhausted their landfills (Earth Works Group, 1989).

The cycle of the lemmings of arctic Norway provides food for thought. Lemmings breed voraciously and eat voraciously in the grasslands of the Norwegian fjords. Early in the cycle there is plenty of food for all of them; their wastes actually fertilize the earth, resulting in increased vegetation for them. However, approximately every 4 years they overpopulate and ravage their territory. In a frenzy, they seek food elsewhere, eventually plunging into the water in an attempt to reach another fjord where food will be available. Most drown or die of exhaustion. A few survive, though, and the cycle begins again (Tobias, 1990).

From this, one can glean the first key factor that makes the Earth a small planet. A small planet is one that is responsible for supporting a rapidly growing population, all of whom, at one level or another, are seeking improved lifestyles promised by the industrial revolution. By 2025 this planet could have over 10 billion people who will want to own their own cars, live in their own houses, and have their own refrigerators, TVs, VCRs, stereos, computers, and robots. In other words, the planet is in a mathematical bind. Like the lemmings, humankind is doing everything possible to squeeze more and more from less and less.

The Earth Is a Closing System

All of this would be well and good, if it were not for the fact that the life-giving and life-supporting processes of the Earth operate in what is essentially a closed ecosystem. According to the laws of thermodynamics, the amount of energy in the universe is constant (conservation); but when energy is transformed from one form to another, it always loses some of its concentration, order, and usefulness (entropy). The more open a system is (that is, the more it can exchange energy, information, and wastes with its environment), the more renewing it can be, thus the less entropy it suffers. This is because an open system is able to import sufficient amounts of energy from its environment to replenish what it loses when transforming its own energy, and it is able to expel the waste products that result from this transformation back into the environment. However, the more closed a system is, the less renewing it can be because it can neither import sufficient quantities of energy to replace its depleted resources, nor dispose of its wastes. Thus the more closed a system is, the more entropy it suffers.

"Open" and "closed" are relative terms. As a system, the Earth has only one significant energy input from its environment—solar flow, the sun. Through photosynthesis, solar energy provides the Earth with the power to feed all of its species; it also provides the basic energy for water and wind cycles. The remainder of the planet's energy is tied directly to terrestrial resources—oil, coal, wood, natural gas, and uranium. Further, the Earth must absorb the wastes generated by the conversion of energy into something useful. These wastes must be buried in the ground, dumped in the water, or spewed into the air. For all but the last 300 years of the 4.5-billion-year history of the Earth, these mechanisms provided a more-than-adequate amount of openness to meet the needs of life on the planet. Father Thomas Berry (1988) says:

> In the natural world there exists an amazing richness of life expression in the ever-renewing cycle of the seasons. There is a minimum of entropy. The inflow of energy and the outflow are such that the process is sustainable over an indefinite period of time. (p. 71)

It has been only during the industrial age that humankind has used the Earth's resources and discharged wastes at rates faster than renewal can take place. This means that the openness the planet once enjoyed has in 300 years—a split second of eternity—almost disappeared. The Earth is now operating essentially as a closed system, an experiment unprecedented in its history. Humankind is beginning to discover that the results of this experiment may be disastrous. Again quoting Father Berry (1988):

> So long as the human process is integral with the processes of nature, the human economy is sustainable in the future. The difficulty comes when the industrial mode of our economy disrupts the natural processes. . . . In such a situation the productivity of the natural world and its life systems is diminished. (p. 71)

Therefore, the second key factor in defining the Earth as a small planet is this: Its natural resources are being expended faster than it can renew them. The population of the planet has engaged willingly in an unprecedented economic experiment, using an ecosystem that has evolved in a beautiful, symphonic balance with its environment for 4.5 billion years. Although it has been known for years that the results for the human species may be nothing short of disastrous if the planet fails to evolve at a rate sufficient to deal with the changes imposed by humankind, the experiment continues at full throttle. Many believe that humans can save themselves with new technologies; however, this promise remains unfulfilled. Real change requires new values and new ways of thinking.

In sum, the Earth is a small planet: one that is limited in the life-sustaining resources needed to support an exponentially increasing population base with ever-increasing economic demands. Such a dilemma puts short-term economic gratification in direct conflict with long-term survival of the species.

The Need for a New Economic Paradigm

What alternatives are available to deal with this dilemma? One solution is to leave it to Nature to solve the problems herself. The Earth will likely be able to renew itself over time, no matter what happens. The problem with this solution is that the Earth renews itself at evolutionary speeds, and the current destruction is occurring at revolutionary speeds. Oil and other terrestrial energy sources will be gone in a matter of decades, and the land, air, and water cannot clean themselves at the rate they are being fouled. Relying on Nature to take care of environmental ills will mean waiting thousands of years while the Earth heals itself. Further, Nature will use mechanisms such as war, starvation, and disease as means for restoring ecological balance. This is not much of a legacy for our children; more positive steps are needed.

Positive steps can be taken in the form of population control. If zero population growth could be achieved on the planet, then environmental problems would be much easier to solve. The authors are certainly proponents of population control, but there is no realistic way to achieve zero population growth any time soon. Optimistic estimates report that the world will have 10 billion people by 2025—the equivalent of four more Chinas being added to the population. Achieving ecological balance by focusing solely on population control is not enough. The fire needs to be extinguished at its source—runaway economic activity.

The facts clearly point to economic activity as a prime source of the Earth's current environmental ills. As discussed earlier, the population exploded in the industrial age (a fact predicted by Malthus in the 18th century). Also, the release of chlorofluorocarbons (CFCs), which didn't even exist until the late 1920s, is primarily responsible for a hole in the Earth's protective ozone layer that is as tall as Mount Everest and as wide as the United States. Further, while trade multiplied 800 times in the industrial age and production multiplied 100 times in the past century, energy use rose 80 times per person, water use rose 36 times per person, the amount of methane in the air doubled, and the amount of carbon dioxide in the air increased by 25% (Clark, 1989).

The lion's share of responsibility for changing the economic paradigm lies with rich nations such as the United States. At a recent presentation concerning this topic, two friends—both top executives for large firms and both concerned about the environment—said that they felt some degree of hopelessness about solving the Earth's environmental problems because the United States had such a small percentage of the world's total population. Yet more than 50% of the Earth's energy is consumed by 15% of the population, the richest (Clark, 1989). The amount of energy that goes into feeding the average American for one day (all of the oil, gas, chemicals, etc.) totals about 250,000 calories (Tobias, 1990). The average American consumes 70 times the water of the average Ghanian (Maurits la Riviere, 1989). Compared to the rest of the world, the developed nations consume 12 times more energy, 10 times more steel, and 15 times more paper (Robertson, 1990).

Further, the same ideals on which economic activity is based are born and grow within these large, successful industrial societies. These nations serve as economic role models for the struggling, developing nations of the world; the free enterprise systems of successful industrial societies are seen as the most direct path to economic prosperity. This is appropriate: No economic institution in a capitalistic democracy can survive if it does not properly serve the interests of its stakeholders, the constituents on whom it relies for economic survival. Thus a corporation operating in a free enterprise system must respond to pressures from its customers, investors, employees, and so on. If these stakeholders demand that corporations be more environmentally responsible, then the corporations will have to comply in order to survive. Halal (1986) makes an excellent case that a "new capitalism" is arising from such pressures.

There is no more logical place to begin economic reform than in the discipline of economics itself. Economic theory forms the foundation of the other business disciplines—finance, accounting, marketing, and management. All of these disciplines fit into the basic closed circular-flow model of economic activity. That is, they all deal with either the production of goods and services, the consumption of goods and services, or the exchange of money that links production and consumption (see Figure 1.1). Therefore, making changes in the way business is practiced will require making changes in the current economic paradigm. (A paradigm is defined as a belief structure or ideology. It is composed of concepts, values, and perceptions shared by the members of society. Some refer to it as a "worldview" [Milbrath, 1989].)

Calls for changes in the economic paradigm are certainly nothing new. A number of economists have proposed new theoretical frameworks that incorporate the Earth's limits. Kenneth E. Boulding published his famous essay, "The Economics of the Coming Spaceship Earth," in 1966; Nicholas Georgescu-Roegen published *The Entropy Law and the Economic Process* in 1971; E. F. Schumacher published *Small Is Beautiful: Economics as if People Mattered* in 1973; Herman E. Daly published *Steady State Economics* in 1977; and Herman E. Daly and John B. Cobb published *For the Common Good* in 1989. Calls for changes in the economic paradigm have come from outside the discipline as well. Sociologist and management scholar Amitai Etzioni, in his 1988 book, *The Moral Dimension: Toward a New Economics,* questions the basic foundations of neoclassical economics and cautions against applying them to management decisions without considering moral and social factors. In his 1986 book, *The New Capitalism,* management scholar William E. Halal contends that there is a trend emerging toward a human economy based on smart growth. Physicist Fritjof Capra, in *The Turning Point* (1983), points out that economic theory is at an impasse because of its unrealistic assumptions about the natural environment and the values that people hold.

At the heart of these criticisms is the current economic paradigm's basic assumption that unlimited economic growth is possible forever. These scholars have developed convincing arguments contending that unlimited economic growth is a fairy tale with the potential for a nightmare ecological ending. For example, Schumacher (1973) says that the unlimited growth assumption leads to business practices that rapidly deplete the planet's resources, destroy the Earth's natural beauty, create mindless tasks for workers, and breed violence by encouraging greed and envy. Daly and Cobb (1989) and Etzioni (1988) argue that a great deal of the excessive egoism found in today's business practices can be tied directly to the unlimited growth assumption. All of these scholars believe that economic thought needs to be changed so that the economic system would no longer be viewed as an entity in and of itself, but rather as a subsystem of the larger social system and ecosystem (see Figure 1.1).

Influencing Strategic Decision Makers

As would be expected, the unrealistic assumption of unlimited economic growth has led to many strategic decisions in business organizations that have resulted in environmental harm. After all, the people who most often apply economic concepts are managers making strategic decisions in business organizations. This same group makes most of the decisions that have the potential to affect the balance of nature. Thus it is within this group that changes in thinking about the relationship between economic activity and ecological sustainability are most critical.

It is important that managers understand that the economic paradigm that they adopt plays a key role in shaping the values they apply to making decisions. Even though traditional economic theories ignore values in all but the most shallow and abstract ways (Daly & Cobb, 1989; Etzioni, 1988), the role of values in making complex strategic choices is well established in other areas of business, such as strategic management, human resource management, and consumer behavior. Values have been clearly shown to influence not only the decisions strategic managers finally make, but also the alternatives and data they choose to consider. Freeman and Gilbert (1988) say in explaining the role of values in strategic decision making:

> The whole point of corporate strategy is to act intentionally in the name of some collective, the corporation. The alternative to corporate strategy is to act randomly or according to the dictates of an outsider. It follows that acting strategically is a matter of acting according to certain values. The values that support a corporate strategy are the most important purposes that we are able to admit to ourselves, or to discover by questioning others. (pp. 51-52)

Values are the key ingredients people use to judge right and wrong. Thus a person's ethical system is, in fact, the sum total of the values he or she holds dear. Further, corporations have ethical systems that are primarily composed of the dominant values of key strategic decision makers in the firm (Goodpaster & Matthews, 1982). Thus it is critical that ethical considerations be incorporated into corporate strategic decision-making processes (Freeman & Gilbert, 1988). Once the planet is integrated into the economic paradigm applied by strategic decision makers, the ethical systems of corporations will be better able to reflect a dominant value for protecting the Earth.

Indeed, many corporations have begun to include environmental protection into their strategic processes. They are making real attempts to internalize the environmental factors still considered externalities in the current economic paradigm. For example, a number of manufacturing firms are currently employing total quality management in efforts to incorporate environmental balance into their strategic decisions. One such firm is 3M, which began implementing its Pollution Prevention Pays program (discussed in more detail in Chapter 9) more than 15 years ago. Tom's of Maine, a manufacturer of personal care products, is another example of a firm that incorporates environmental responsibility into its strategic decision-making processes; its mission's guiding principle explicitly states that it is committed to earning a profit within the Earth's environmental limits (Earth Works Group, 1989).

The Plan of the Book

This book is divided into three parts. The second chapter of this part provides a summary of the environmental issues faced by the planet. We examine how the conversion of natural resources into economic outputs in order to satisfy the economic desires of an ever-increasing population base has led to problems such as global warming, ozone depletion, water pollution and depletion, deforestation, oil and mineral depletion, land degradation, and so on.

Part 2 examines conceptual frameworks relevant to understanding what a small planet is and how it relates to economic growth and managerial decision making. This section draws on information from such diverse disciplines as physics, environmental science, biology, economics, management, psychology, sociology, and ethics. In Chapter 3, we discuss the Earth as a living system, and we examine such topics as thermodynamics and energy science. By introducing these topics, we hope to make readers aware that management decisions need to be consistent with the limits of the Earth, because that is their venue. In Chapter 4, we discuss the role values play in complex human decision making. Because strategic decisions represent the most complex and multidimensional decisions made by business managers, we feel it is important to provide managers with a clear picture of how their values influence their strategic choices. In Chapter 5, we discuss some of the basic fallacies of the current economic paradigm and present some of the ideas being forwarded about a new, more environmentally sensitive economic paradigm.

The final part of the book focuses on how business managers can adapt their strategic decision-making approaches to include a small-planet way of thinking and acting. In Chapter 6, we discuss the emerging management paradigm, and we make some suggestions for incorporating the planet into that paradigm. In Chapter 7, we present values for a small planet. These are values that, if adopted by strategic decision makers, can be instrumental in helping managers make choices that are compatible with the ecosystem. Chapter 8 focuses on the growing movements among organizational stakeholders (including consumers, investors, and the political/legal system) demanding environmental responsibility from organizations. In the final chapter of the book (Chapter 9), we present the concept of "sustainability strategies," which are strategies designed to integrate the ecological needs of the planet with the long-term economic needs of the firm.

Chapter 2

The Issue Wheel

> Gaia said to William, Economic disaster is closing in on your species from all sides. Gas and oil will soon be in short supply. The reserves of precious metals and coal are being exhausted. Tropical rainforests are vanishing, while topsoil is eroding away. The human population is increasing by billions. The atmosphere is becoming denser with carbon dioxide. Your fossil fuel emissions are accumulating in the upper atmosphere, trapping the sun's irradiation and thus warming up the entire planet. That might work for hothouse orchids, but not for human beings. Meanwhile, the problems associated with hundreds of millions of people stuck without the basic energy needs are rapidly escalating. (Tobias, 1990, p. 198)

This passage from Michael Tobias's *Voice of the Planet* succinctly summarizes the Earth's environmental problems. The Earth is in a vicious cycle similar to that of a roulette wheel. As the spinning wheel awaits the random, chance landing of the ball, so the spinning Earth awaits the occurrence of the next environmental disaster. When and where will the next disastrous oil spill occur? When and where will there be another Love Canal, Times Beach, Bhopal, or Chernobyl? When will another Chico Mendes die defending the rain forests? Which pesticide, herbicide, fungicide, or rodenticide will be the next to be declared carcinogenic? How many people will die this year of cancer or respiratory illness contracted on the job? 'Round and 'round it goes, where it stops nobody knows.

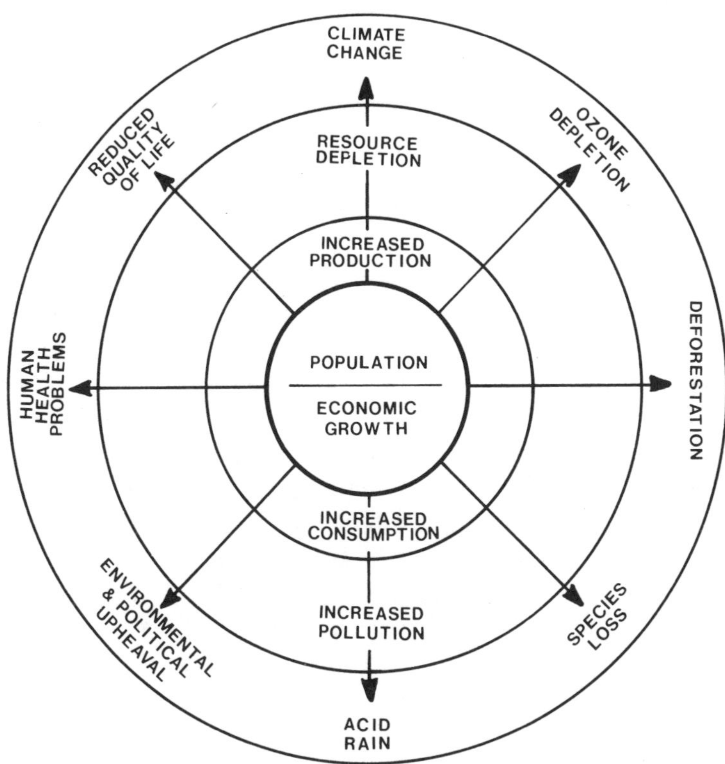

Figure 2.1. The Issue Wheel.

In this chapter, we examine this issue wheel. A wheel is a series of concentric support systems that radiate from the hub out to the rim. The environmental issues that we face today are much like this; they begin at a central source and radiate out into the larger ecosystem. We will look at the process whereby unlimited economic growth and population growth are acting together to create far-reaching concentric problems in the ecosystem. As Figure 2.1 depicts, the world's rapidly increasing population and the belief in the potential for unlimited economic growth lead directly to increased production and consumption. As humankind incessantly produces and consumes, it continues to deplete its resources and to foul its nest with its own wastes and pollutants. The resulting problems include environmental catastrophe, poor air and water quality, loss of species, climate change, land degradation, and a lower quality of life, now and for posterity.

Most readers are probably aware of the current environmental problems. The Worldwatch Institute publishes its *State of the World* report each year detailing the most serious environmental issues. *Time, National Geographic, Newsweek, Scientific American, Fortune,* and scores of other national and international publications have all dedicated special issues to the Earth. Turner Broadcasting, PBS, and the major networks have committed vast time and resources documenting the planet's environmental ills. Earth Day 1990 was one of the most successful public awareness events in the history of the environmental movement, culminating 20 years of often frustrating work. Books such as the Earth Works Group's *50 Simple Things You Can Do to Save the Earth* (1989) and Jeffrey Hollender's *How to Make the World a Better Place* (1990) have been national best-sellers.

In this chapter we will try to present readers with a coherent summary of existing and potential environmental problems in a way that will elucidate the nature of these problems, the contribution of business activity to these problems, and the complexity of the interrelationships among these problems. Strategic decision makers don't need to be environmental scientists, but they need to be aware of the issues so that they can be prepared to take appropriate actions.

Population and the Growth Mentality at the Hub

We demonstrated in Chapter 1 that the Earth's population is growing at a phenomenal rate, with estimates ranging as high as 14 billion by the year 2025. Well-known environmentalist Garrett Hardin (1968) spoke to this problem more than 20 years ago in his classic article, "The Tragedy of the Commons," in which he graphically describes the dire consequences to the planet that may result from unlimited population growth. He demonstrates that an exponentially growing population will eventually use and degrade the natural environment to the point that scarcity of the Earth's limited life-supporting resources (which he calls the "commons") will finally begin to affect humankind's ability to survive as a species.

An important point concerning population growth is realizing that overpopulation is not a problem of space. A recent letter to the editor of the Johnson City, Tennessee, *Press* blasted environmentalists as nothing but doomsayers. The writer based his argument on the fact that all the people in the world could fit into Carter County, Tennessee. He was right, of course. Everyone on Earth can fit in a space of 1,000 square miles with 5 square feet for each person. The problem, however, is not lack of space, but the fact that it takes a vast quantity of natural resources to keep everyone alive and to absorb all of their wastes (Ornstein & Ehrlich, 1990). Thus overpopulation occurs "when [an area] can't be maintained without rapidly depleting nonrenewable resources . . . and without degrading the capacity of the environment to support the population" (Ehrlich & Ehrlich, 1990, pp. 38-39).

This point is critical because it is often assumed that overpopulation is solely a Third World problem. In fact, developed nations like the United States, western European countries, and Japan are overpopulated because they are depleting their soil, water, and environment, and because they are required to import a high percentage of the natural resources and energy used to power their economies. For example, Japan, with a population of 125 million in an area the size of California, imports almost all of its energy and natural resources as well as about half of its food. The United States imports about half of its oil and is rapidly depleting its soil and water resources. For example, it was recently reported that by the year 2020, population growth in the Chesapeake Bay watershed of the United States (which includes parts of Maryland, Virginia, and Pennsylvania, as well as Washington DC) may offset the environmental improvement that area is currently experiencing because of better sewage treatment and pollution control (LeBlanc, 1991).

Ehrlich and Ehrlich (1990) give an excellent example of overpopulation problems in developed nations with what they call the "Netherlands Fallacy." In 1989, *Forbes* magazine presented the Netherlands (a densely populated developed nation) as an example of a country that was not overpopulated. However, the Netherlands imports massive tonnages of various foodstuffs and 100% of its iron, tin, bauxite, copper, and many other minerals; further, it extracts most of its freshwater from the Rhine River, which flows in from countries to the north. Until productive natural gas fields were discovered in the 1970s, the country also imported all of its energy; these gas fields will be exhausted in about 20 years, and the Netherlands will again be 100% dependent on energy imports. Ehrlich and Ehrlich (1990) say, "The Netherlands can support 1031 people per square mile only because the rest of the world does not" (p. 39).

Although overpopulation exists in all corners of the globe, population growth is occurring fastest in the poorer nations of the world (i.e., India, China, and many African nations), where approximately 75% of the Earth's people live (Commoner, 1990). The poorer nations are doubling their populations about every 29 years, while the richer nations are doubling their populations about every 120 years. This gap is likely to widen in the foreseeable future because the age of the population in underdeveloped countries is much younger than in developed nations. More than 40% of the population of poorer nations is under the age of 15, meaning that they have most of their reproductive years ahead of them (Ehrlich & Ehrlich, 1990). That is why 90% of the world's population increases in the next century are expected in the Third World (Toufexis, 1989).

The next factor in the hub of the issue wheel is unlimited economic growth. As we discussed briefly in the last chapter and will discuss in more depth later in the book, economic growth is not sustainable forever because of the limits of the planet. Yet the potential for unlimited economic growth is a key belief that pervades current free market economic systems; the myth that everyone can have all the material wealth they want forever is still a dominant element in the economic paradigm.

Peter Senge (1990), a management professor at MIT and a noted consultant for some of the largest corporations in the United States, says, "For most American business people the best rate of growth is fast, faster, fastest. Yet virtually all natural systems, from ecosystems to animals to organizations, have intrinsically optimal rates of growth. The optimal rate is far less than the fastest possible growth" (p. 62).

When economic theory was first developed by Adam Smith and others in the early days of the industrial revolution, unlimited growth was a relatively harmless assumption because very few people in very few nations were actually involved in significant economic activity; it certainly seemed as if there was plenty for everyone. However, rapid population growth and the increased number of nations involved in high levels of economic activity since that time have changed the situation drastically. Further, the recent fall of the iron curtain means that even more people in more nations have plans to become a part of the economic-growth landscape. Poland, Hungary, Bulgaria, and Czechoslovakia have entered the age of democratic capitalism, a unified Germany has emerged, and many of the republics that were once under the Leninist fist of the Soviet Union are now intent on becoming free market economies. And, it seems inevitable that even China, a country with a population of 1.2 billion, will embody democratic capitalism sometime in the future. Nations throughout the world are now saying, "We want to play, too. We want a piece of the pie." If there are 10 billion people in 2025 and most of them are living in growth-oriented economic systems (which could certainly occur if current population, economic, and political trends continue), the planet will not be able to manage the stress without making significant changes to business practices. The Earth does not have the natural capital (fossil fuels, groundwater, clean air, forests, etc.) to absorb an exponential increase in humankind's assault. Humankind is now faced squarely with the need to evaluate what kind of economic growth and how much economic growth it wants.

Resource Depletion and Pollution Radiating From the Hub

We discussed previously the fact that the Earth is a relatively closed system with little ability to import inputs or export outputs beyond its boundaries. Thus the increased production and consumption associated with a growing population in a growth-oriented society flies directly in the face of ecological balance. Resources are being depleted at increasingly rapid rates, and the environment is being degraded by an overflow of pollutants and waste products. Frosch and Gallopoulos (1989) estimate that if humans are consuming in 2030 at the same rate the average U.S. citizen consumes today, "Critical natural resources would last less than a decade. On the waste side of the ledger . . . [humankind] would generate 400 billion tons of solid waste every year—enough to bury greater Los Angeles 100 meters deep" (p. 144). In this section we examine the problems of resource depletion and pollution more closely (see Figure 2.1).

Depleting Resources

Resources are so important because, ultimately, they are the only capital humans have. They are the basic source of material wealth, financial wealth, and psychological wealth. Commenting on this, Ornstein and Ehrlich (1990) say:

> Humanity is living largely on its "capital"—nonrenewable resources. . . . The capital that we inherited included fossil fuels, high grade mineral ores, rich agricultural soils, groundwater stored up during the ice ages, and above all, the millions of species that inhabit the Earth along with us. Our total inheritance took billions of years to assemble; it is being squandered in decades. . . . Humanity is rapidly and wastefully depleting fossil fuels before satisfactory substitute energy supplies have been developed and, in the process, seriously damaging its environment. . . . We are a nouveau riche species struggling to become nouveau broke. (pp. 45-46)

Environmental scientist H. T. Odum (1990) points out that the economic value normally assigned to natural capital is the reverse of its value in nature. He says that the more work nature has to do, the less work humans have to do in converting the resource. A mature redwood tree takes hundreds of years to develop and provides tremendous amounts of oxygen, but it takes little effort to burn it for fuel or to convert it into a deck or hot tub.

One of the planet's most precious resources, forests, are disappearing at an astonishing rate. This is especially true in the tropics, where a total of almost 40 million acres a year is being lost (Postel, 1988). Senator Albert Gore is fond of pointing out that all of the world's military might would be aimed at a giant alien monster from outer space if it were tromping down the rain forests at a rate of one football field per second (approximately 45,000 square feet). Yet that is the rate at which these forests are disappearing. Ethiopia's forest cover has declined from 30% of its land to 1% of its land in 40 years. India's forest cover has declined from more than 50% to around 14% since 1900. In Brazil, where Chico Mendes died protecting what he called the "lungs of the planet," 20 million acres are being cut annually. In the tropics, only one tree is being planted for every 10 cut (McNeill, 1989). With these forests go much of the oxygen needed to breathe and the habitats of most of the Earth's species: Economic activities are the primary culprit in this problem. The forests are being harvested and shipped to nations like Japan and the United States where they are converted into wood for furniture, homes, and other products; forest clearing is also occurring in order to convert the land to farming and raising livestock.

Nonrenewable fossil fuels are also being exhausted at incredible rates. Eighty-eight percent of total global energy is derived from coal, oil, and natural gas (Gibbons, Blair, & Gwin, 1989). Problems associated with the use of fossil fuels are probably most evident for oil. As current sources of oil are exhausted, new sources are sought. These new sources are invariably less accessible, and thus more costly both economically and ecologically. The cost of oil production has increased exponentially, doubling every 15 years. If substitutes for oil are not found, massive shortages and price increases are likely to occur, beginning around 2020; these shortages and price increases will be so great that they will lead to a permanent energy crisis that will only worsen with time (Commoner, 1990).

The reserves of topsoil are also being consumed at unsustainable rates. It is estimated that 24 to 26 billion tons more topsoil are depleted every year than are replenished by nature (Ehrlich & Ehrlich, 1990). Topsoil loss is a multidimensional problem that involves overcultivation, salinization, use of chemical fertilizers, and urbanization. Humans in general and the agricultural industry in particular face a real challenge in the next century—trying to feed twice the current population with less environmental damage (Crosson & Rosenberg, 1989).

Agriculture is a major contributor to yet another resource problem—the loss of groundwater, which is essentially nonrenewable in the short run. Groundwater provides a significant part of the drinking water in the world (it provides about 50% of the United States' drinking water) as well as being a major irrigation source for croplands. Groundwater is being used much faster than it is being replaced on the assumption that there will always be new sources. Thirty-three hundred cubic kilometers are withdrawn annually for irrigation purposes: six times the annual flow of the Mississippi River (Crosson & Rosenberg, 1989). Irrigation is primarily responsible for the rapid depletion of the Ogallala Aquifer under the Great Plains of the United States as well as the aquifers under the San Joaquin Valley of California. These aquifers provide water for the major farmlands in the United States. Aquifer depletion is also occurring in other parts of the globe; for example, depleting aquifers are predicted to lead to water shortages in 450 of the 644 cities in China by the year 2000 (Ehrlich & Ehrlich, 1990).

Increasing Pollution

So there is little doubt that humankind is overspending its natural capital. But where does it go? The answer, of course, is that it goes into the air, the water, and the ground in the form of environmentally degrading pollution. These are human wastes: Although human wastes are normally thought of in terms of personal biological processes, it is time to expand that term to account for the incredible amount of "stuff" emitted into the environment as a result of consumption and production processes.

Let us begin by examining air pollution. Fossil fuel burning, biomass burning (i.e., burning the rain forests to clear them for grazing land), agricultural activities, and declining forest cover are infusing massive quantities of toxins into the atmosphere every day. In 1987, industrial activity alone (not including automobile emissions or agriculture) was responsible for the release of 2.7 billion pounds of toxic gases into the air (Faltermayer, 1989).

During the industrial age, there has been an unprecedented increase in the presence of potentially dangerous trace gases in the atmosphere; trace gases are those that make up a very small proportion of the total atmospheric gases. Examples of dangerous trace gases that are increasing include sulfur dioxide (SO_2) (which has increased from .03 parts per billion to 50 parts per billion), nitrogen oxides (NO and NO_2) (which have increased from .001 parts per billion to 50 parts per billion), nitrous oxide (N_2O) (which is expected to increase from 310 parts per billion to 350 parts per billion by the year 2030), methane (CH_4) (which is expected to increase from 1,700 parts per billion to 2,500 parts per billion by the year 2030), and various chlorofluorocarbons (CFCs) (which currently account for 3 parts per billion but will likely grow to 6 parts per billion by 2030). In the meantime the hydroxyl radical (OH) exists in concentrations of only .00001 parts per billion; however, it serves as a primary filtering agent for the atmosphere. Recent data indicate that OH may very well be decreasing; if this occurs, the atmosphere's ability to cleanse itself could be seriously affected (Graedel & Crutzen, 1989).

By far the most prominent trace gas in the atmosphere is carbon dioxide (CO_2) (at 350,000 parts per billion); it is also the trace gas that is increasing most rapidly (Graedel & Crutzen, 1989; Lemonick, 1989). Each year 6 billion tons of CO_2 are released into the atmosphere (Earth Works Group, 1989). The primary responsibility for CO_2 emissions lies with industrialized nations; for example, CO_2 in the United States is emitted at a rate of 5 tons per person per year, which is five times the world's average per capita rate (Weiner, 1990). A great deal of the excessive increases in CO_2 in the atmosphere during the industrial age can be attributed to the reduction in the Earth's vegetation due to increasing population and economic growth. Because plants take carbon dioxide out of the air, declining vegetation means that the ecosystem has less ability to remove CO_2 (Commoner, 1990).

Humankind is being no kinder to its water. Besides using water at an irreplaceable rate, toxic chemicals and other waste products are being poured into the water as if it were a personal dump. The notion that people can put what they want into the waterways regardless of who is downstream has led to a major decline in the availability of safe drinking water throughout the world. Human and animal wastes, agricultural wastes, and industrial wastes are dumped into the Earth's aboveground and underground waterways (Maurits la Riviere, 1989). At least 10% (17,000) of the U.S. waterways, and probably many more, are seriously polluted, and carry restrictions on drinking and fishing uses (*ABC News, June 13, 1989*). In the 16 months following the Valdez oil spill, more than 6,000,000 gallons of oil were spilled into U.S. waterways (*CNN News, August 2, 1990*). The Mississippi River below Baton Rouge, Louisiana, has been declared the "cancer corridor" because of the high levels of carcinogenic chemicals discharged into it by the hundreds of chemical plants along the river. Toxins are injected into groundwater as well as surface water. The U.S. Geological Survey tested more than 100,000 wells in the agricultural regions of the nation in the early 1980s and found that there have been dangerous increases in nitrates (from fertilizers) as well as other toxic chemicals (Commoner, 1990).

The wastes that are not spewed into the air or poured into the water are buried in the ground. Americans send enough aluminum to landfills every 3 months to rebuild the U.S. commercial air fleet. Sixteen billion disposable diapers, 220 million tires, and 2 billion disposable razors are buried every year. Eighty percent of the solid wastes go to 6,000 landfills, most of which are full to the brim. Three thousand dumps closed in the past 5 years, and 2,000 more are expected to close by 1993 (Langone,

1989). In Tennessee alone, 85 of the 95 landfills are full or almost full.

In addition to the landfill problem, there is the problem of burying toxic chemical and nuclear wastes. The Department of Energy estimates that it will cost Americans $100 billion to safely bury the billions of pounds of weapons-related nuclear wastes that have been stored in barrels in the past 40 years in the United States (this may be a very conservative estimate because no permanent burial site for nuclear wastes has yet been located). There are more than 1,000,000 barrels of high-level nuclear wastes currently waiting for burial; if laid end-to-end, they could reach from Seattle to New York (*CNN News, August 6, 1990*). Also, there are 600 billion pounds of toxic chemicals buried every year in the United States. These chemicals are buried in such places as Emelle, Alabama, the nation's largest toxic landfill, where 1.6 billion pounds are buried each year. When it started operating in 1977, Emelle was ballyhooed as the perfect toxic waste dump because of the nature of the soil in the area. However, within a decade wastes began appearing in groundwater; in 1989, Governor Guy Hunt, a conservative Republican, stood at the gate of the landfill and tried to bar shipments of PCB-laden dirt from Texas and Arkansas (White, 1989). Alabama is now attempting to institute a two-tier waste-disposal tax structure to discourage further toxic waste imports.

The Wheel of Misfortune

As can be seen from the previous discussion, humankind is spending its natural resources more rapidly than they can be replenished and polluting its air, water, and land in the process. In short, people are bankrupting themselves of the natural capital that they depend on for survival. There are several environmental problems that are the results of these resource depleting and polluting activities. Let's examine some of these environmental problems, which are exhibited on the outer rim of the issue wheel (Figure 2.1).

Probably the most visible results of this natural capital exploitation are highly publicized environmental and political upheavals. Environmental disasters read like a list of nations, towns, and waterways on a perverted guided tour: hundreds of oil wells set ablaze by Iraqi soldiers in Kuwait; major oil spills at Monterey, California; Valdez, Alaska; and Galveston Bay, Texas; chemical disasters at Love Canal, New York; Times Beach, Missouri; Sacramento River, California; and Bhopal, India; nuclear meltdowns at Three Mile Island, Pennsylvania; and Chernobyl, USSR. In addition to these man-made natural disasters, there are the numerous political confrontations associated with scarce resources, especially petroleum. The Arab oil embargo was imposed on nations who supported Israel in 1973, and the recent war with Iraq occurred because Iraq invaded Kuwait in an attempt to control the world's oil supply. But even though these environmental and political upheavals became major media events for a time, they are only the tip of the iceberg in terms of events that cause environmental problems for the planet. For example, more motor oil is deposited into U.S. waterways every year than was spilled by the Exxon Valdez. As Ornstein and Ehrlich (1990) point out, single spectacular events capture people's attention, but insidious long-term problems are often ignored.

One of these insidious problems is climate change. The increase of trace gases in the atmosphere (as mentioned earlier) increases the Earth's potential for trapping heat near the surface and may result in rising temperatures now and into the future. It is believed that CO_2 comprises approximately 50% of the Earth's "greenhouse gases" (Earth Works Group, 1989), and the remainder is composed of methane, CFCs, and so on. Interest in this problem is fueled by the fact that the global temperature average for 1990 was the highest ever recorded, and that the seven warmest years since 1880 occurred from 1980 through 1990 (Vital signs, 1991). Although there is no debate over the potential for the "greenhouse effect," there is certainly debate over whether it will actually occur, to what degree, and over what period of time. Will the average temperature rise eight degrees or only one degree? Will it take 50 years or 150 years

(Schneider, 1989)? The most important question, however, may be whether or not humankind can afford to wait and see. Is it worth watching New Orleans sink into the Gulf of Mexico or seeing the fertile midwestern farmlands become arid deserts in order to have proof?

Stratospheric (upper atmosphere) ozone (O_3) depletion is another serious atmospheric condition. This depletion is primarily linked to one particular family of chemicals, CFCs, which are used in air-conditioning, refrigeration, propellants, and solvents. The stratospheric ozone layer protects the Earth from the ultraviolet radiation of the sun. Without this protection, there is likely to be an increase in skin cancer, a reduction in human immune system efficiency, as well as potentially devastating effects on the food chain (Graedel & Crutzen, 1989). The first hole in the ozone was discovered over Antarctica by British scientists in 1985. Since then, scientists have also documented an area of ozone depletion over the Arctic which has the potential for a one percent decline per day under the right climatic conditions (Stammer, 1989). It is believed that springtime levels of ozone over the Antarctic have declined 50% in the past decade with a 2% to 10% decline over the Arctic (Graedel & Crutzen, 1989). In April, 1991, the Environmental Protection Agency announced that NASA studies had found that the upper-level ozone over the United States (as well as parts of Europe) is depleting at twice the rate previously believed; between 4% and 5% has already been depleted (McCully, 1991). This means that the number of deaths expected from skin cancer in the United States could double; an additional 200,000 people may die from skin cancer over the next 50 years if this trend is not reversed (Accelerated ozone loss cancer threat, 1991).

Whereas ozone is necessary in the upper atmosphere, it causes smog when it exists in excess in the lower atmosphere. Smog occurs when various trace gases react with solar radiation in the lower atmosphere "to produce reactive gases that can be destructive to living organisms" (Graedel & Crutzen, 1989, p. 61); thus, as fossil fuels and other energy sources are burned to power the economy, more smog is created. Ozone is the most prominent of these reactive gases; lower atmosphere ozone levels have increased between four and 10 times in the past century. Further, this problem is expanding beyond urban, industrial areas into the more remote regions of the Earth; national parks in the United States such as the Great Smoky Mountains and the Grand Canyon are experiencing serious declines in visibility levels due to smog. Smog has been related to eye and lung problems in human beings as well as to the damage of foliage and agricultural crops (Graedel & Crutzen, 1989).

Further, not all of these pollutants stay in the air. Certain trace gases have water soluble molecules and thus mix with the moisture in the air and return as acid rain, a term that describes acidic snow, dew, and fog, as well as rain. Nitrogen oxides and sulfur dioxide, released into the air because of the burning of fossil fuels for industrial activity, transportation, and so on, go through chemical reactions in the atmosphere and are converted into nitric acid and sulfuric acid. These acids mix readily with water molecules and plunge back to Earth in the form of precipitation. The result has been acidification of lakes and streams, declines in diversity and number of fish in certain regions, and destruction of forests (Graedel & Crutzen, 1989; The acid rain report, 1989). Thirteen states in the United States, especially in the Northeast, the Appalachians, and the upper Michigan Peninsula, have experienced serious acidic pollution problems (MacKenzie & ElAshry, 1989; The acid rain report, 1989). Mt. Mitchell, North Carolina, the highest peak in the United States east of the Mississippi River, has lost many of its trees, and this same effect is now being seen on lower peaks in North Carolina and Tennessee; Canada has also been hard hit. Acid rain is expected to cost Europe $30 billion worth of wood every year for the next century (Vital signs, 1991). The emerging democracies of central and eastern Europe may have the worst acid rain problem of all. For example, two out of every three trees in Czechoslovakia are dead or dying because of acid rain (*CNN News, July 28, 1990*).

Many scientists believe that the worst problem created by polluting and resource depleting activities is declining biodiversity. Noted biologist Edward O. Wilson (1989) says, "In one sense the loss of diversity is the most important process of environmental change . . . because it is the only process that is wholly irreversible" (p. 108). Of the 4 million to 30 million species currently inhabiting the planet, some scientists predict that 100 species a day will be driven to extinction in the next 30 years because of economic growth activities. Most of the extinction is occurring in the tropics, home to between 50% and 80% of these species. Extinction is nothing new; ninety-nine percent of the species that have inhabited the Earth are now extinct. However, the current rate is 1,000 times higher than that of any other period in history (Easterbrook, 1989; Linden, 1989). Also, approximately 25% of pharmaceuticals are obtained from tropical plants (Linden, 1989), and most of the Earth's 75,000 plants with edible parts exist in the tropics (Wilson, 1989). Given these statistics and the fact that only 1.4 million species have even been classified by biologists, it seems that carelessly shepherding these species into extinction without even discovering them, much less determining their usefulness, makes little sense.

There are also human health costs that are directly related to the Earth's depletion and pollution problems. Many of these costs have already been mentioned: cancer, malnutrition, radiation poisoning, and destruction of lifesaving pharmaceuticals. Add to these the respiratory problems (such as chronic bronchitis and emphysema) that are associated with air pollution, and the dysentery, cholera, and other diseases that are associated with unsafe drinking water, and you get a clear picture of how human health is being affected by the growth mentality.

One of the places where the human costs are most apparent is the workplace. For example, accidents with and long-term exposure to toxic substances contribute significantly to the fact that workers in the oil, chemical, and nuclear industries have a life expectancy 10 years below that of the average American (Mazzocchi, 1990). Cancer in the workplace is a particularly insidious health problem related to pollution. Worker exposure to carcinogenic materials is a long-standing and well-documented problem (Stead & Stead, 1980, 1986). Asbestos was suspected of causing lung cancer as early as 1930 (Epstein, 1975). Chemicals such as arsenic, vinyl chloride, chromium, nickel, and benzene are often found in the workplace and have been identified as carcinogens (Cole & Goldman, 1975). Epidemiological evidence suggests that cancers of the lung, liver, urinary bladder, skin, hematopoietic, and lymphatic systems are related to occupation (Swanson, 1988).

There is, however, widespread disagreement about the incidence levels of cancer caused by occupational factors. In fact, determining incidence levels of cancer is a complex and inexact process at best. The best available data show that about 4% of all cancer is directly caused by occupational exposure to carcinogens (6% for males and 2% for females) (Peto, 1985). However, when this figure is extended to include cases in which occupational carcinogens play a partial as well as direct role in the chances of employees developing cancer (for example, when an industrial carcinogen reacts synergistically with tobacco smoke), then it is believed that between 20% and 38% of the total incidence of cancer is occupationally related (Bridbord, Decoufle, & Fraumeni, 1978). Regardless of whether the proportion is 4% or 38%, the numbers are significant because cancer accounts for hundreds of thousands of deaths each year.

If people ask themselves if economic growth is something that improves their quality of life, their initial reaction would likely be that it certainly does. But a closer look at this question reveals that unlimited material consumption is not all that it is cracked up to be. Abraham Maslow pointed out years ago that material growth does not necessarily bring personal fulfillment on the job or in life. People's personal happiness is based on meaningful social relationships and sufficient opportunities to grow personally and spiritually.

Paul Wachtel (1989) makes an excellent case for more not necessarily meaning better or happier. He points out that from 1958 until 1980, the proportion of air-conditioner use in the U.S. population rose 484%, freezer use rose 134%, clothes dryer use rose 356%, and dishwasher use rose 743%. (Remember this is proportionate use, meaning that the percentage of the population having access to these appliances rose by these astounding figures.) If it were ever going to be proven that increased material growth means more happiness, then this was the time to prove it. But guess what? People were *not* happier. In fact, people perceived that their quality of life declined during the period Wachtel addresses. The 1970s are viewed as a time of stagflation, when growth rates were low and prices (especially energy prices) were high. President Reagan won a landslide election over President Carter in 1980 by asking, "Are you better-off than you were four years ago?" Everyone answered no, and rushed to elect a new man—even though real income was actually up 16%. Why? How can people feel worse-off when they are economically better-off? Wachtel (1989) says that such feelings are due to the growth mentality, which causes high levels of psychological stress. Two cars were a luxury for the past generation, but they have become a necessity for the current generation. If parents bought their dream house in their 40s, then their children feel that they should be able to buy theirs in their 20s. On and on it goes until this penchant for material consumption knocks the wind out of psychological well-being. People are not as happy with their lifestyles as they think.

Kanter and Mirvis (1989) document an American society that is cynical and disillusioned. Lester Milbrath (1990) calls growth "a false god," and Fritjof Capra (1975) warns that just as a person traveling east will eventually end up in the west, the incessant accumulation of economic wealth will eventually lead to a poor quality of life.

Conclusions

Population and the unlimited growth mentality react together as two equally powerful tug-of-war teams matched on a dirt field with a muddy pond between them. They pull at each other with all of their might. As they continue the endless cycles of digging in, sliding to the edge of the pond, and pulling away, they destroy the dry ground under their feet until it slowly absorbs the water from the pond. Long before the end of the contest, each team is likely to be mired in grime and mud. As the now pressing questions concerning how much population growth and economic growth humankind can afford are pondered, try to imagine a world in which 10 billion people on the planet enjoy the same growth-oriented lifestyle of the average U.S. citizen with all the ecological and psychological baggage that this entails. Then it becomes clear that, in fact, it may not be advisable for everyone to be as "well-off" as the average U.S. citizen, even if it were possible. As we have shown, the Earth and its human inhabitants simply cannot afford it. Posterity cannot be risked for short-term economic gain. People are not any happier (and in fact they are less happy) despite increased economic wealth. The current economic activities are dangerously affecting the air people breathe, the water people drink, the land people live on, and the other living species of the Earth. Donald Trump told Larry King of CNN that business is all a game. Well, if that is true, and no doubt many believe that it is, then some new rules are sorely needed—rules that will protect planet Earth, the household of all living things.

PART TWO

Framework for a Small Planet

Yes, some new rules are needed. A new framework is necessary; one that will allow managers to engage in successful business activities within the sustainable limits of the Earth. We visualize such a framework as consisting of three components: first, a basic understanding of the laws of the ecosystem as they apply to business activity; second, an understanding of how the values held by decision makers in business organizations influence their strategic choices; and third, an understanding of new economic assumptions that can provide the foundation for values that allow strategic managers to include the planet in their decisions. Such a framework will provide strategic managers with the knowledge they need to be more aware of the ecological effects of their decisions, and it will allow them to adopt and apply economic values that are more compatible with the ecosystem. In this section we explore the following three components: We examine the Earth as a living system subject to the laws of nature; we examine the role that values play in strategic decisions; and we present a brief discussion of a new, environmentally sensitive economic paradigm.

Chapter 3

Management Happens on Earth

Strategic managers are frequently eyewitnesses to the environmental impacts of their decisions. Some of the first people on the scene at Three Mile Island and Valdez, Alaska, were executives (although Lawrence Rawl, Exxon's Chief Executive Officer (CEO), refused to visit Valdez immediately). Warren Anderson, CEO of Union Carbide, went directly to India after the accident at Bhopal and was arrested when he got there. Strategic managers see smokestacks, drainpipes, and emission statistics on a regular basis. All this exposure should make one fact obvious to these managers: They are earthbound in practicing their profession.

The problem is that business managers are trained to focus on only one of the Earth's many subsystems—the economic subsystem (see Figure 1.1). However, the economic subsystem does not exist in isolation. Long-term economic well-being can only exist within an ecosystem that has sufficient energy and resources to support it. Thus strategic managers interested in making decisions that are compatible with the long-term survival of the human species need a basic understanding of the living system called Earth. The purpose of this chapter is to provide such an understanding. We will examine the Earth as a living system, discuss the relationships between the laws of thermodynamics and economic activity, and examine the relationship between industrial activity and energy consumption.

The Earth Is a Living System

A basic mystery for humankind is defining life itself. It is like trying to solve a series of riddles with no answers. Where does life come from? Where does it go? Why can it be destroyed but not created? Science and philosophy spring from humankind's quest to solve these riddles, but so far, more questions have been generated than answers. Dictionaries provide little insight; they define life as that which distinguishes the living from the dead. Our favorite definition of life comes from Michael Tobias (1990) who says, "Life is the energy that organizes matter into self-portraits" (p. 50).

Though people may not be able to define it, they know life when they see it. The difference between alive and not alive is fairly obvious in most cases. Because life can't be defined but is usually easy to recognize, scientific inquiries into its nature are typically restricted to delineating those characteristics that help to distinguish the living from the nonliving. For example, it is known that living things have boundaries (qualities that distinguish them from their environments); process matter, energy, and information; maintain individual identity; consist of living parts; and live in collectives with others of their kind (Lovelock, 1990).

What Is a Living System?

The term *living system* refers to something that exhibits the characteristics of life. A living system does not need to be alive in the biological sense, but it should have biological functions such as birth, death, and reproduction. A living system is open, meaning it exchanges information, matter, and/or energy with its environment in order to counteract uncertainty and decay. It receives feedback from its environment that helps to balance inputs and outputs so that it can maintain a dynamic equilibrium. A living system has some purpose, goal, or final state that it seeks (Van Gigch, 1978).

A living system is complex; it is composed of a finite number of component subsystems that process information, matter, and/or energy. These component subsystems are highly interdependent and cannot be treated as isolated entities. A living system is an irreducible whole; when its component subsystems break down, its survival is threatened. Further, a living system displays certain properties that could never be anticipated by analyzing its component subsystems; it is different from the sum of its parts (Van Gigch, 1978).

Systems exist at different levels of physical, social, and/or spiritual complexity; thus they can be arranged in hierarchies. Dozens of authors have postulated various systems hierarchies (often called chains of being) (Wilber, 1985). Kenneth Boulding (1956) points out that these hierarchical arrangements help people to understand that there aren't just systems; there is a "system of systems" (p. 202). E. F. Schumacher (1977) elucidates this point further, saying that various systems can be understood only if their "level of being is fully taken into account" (p. 14). Living systems are, of course, of a higher order than nonliving systems. A number of hierarchies have been proposed. J. G. Miller says that cells are at the lowest level of living systems, followed by organs, organisms, groups, organizations, societies, and, finally, supranational systems (Van Gigch, 1978). Boulding (1956) also begins with cells, but follows with plants, animals, humans, social systems, and transcendental systems. Each level both includes and transcends the previous level. For example, animals include the basic properties of plants but are also more conscious of their environment and thus better able to react to it. Humans have the environmental consciousness of animals but are also self-aware: They can set goals for themselves and reflect on their experiences. Organizations are collectives of humans but have the potential to harmonize the conflicting goals of individual members into synergistic cooperative efforts that can achieve very ambitious outcomes (Schumacher, 1977; Van Gigch, 1978).

Earth: The System of Systems

The Earth is a living system that both encompasses and transcends the matter, plants, animals, people, and organizations that make it up. From its environment it imports sunlight that provides the energy for resource development and life itself. The planet's survival depends on the delicate interaction between the atmosphere, oceans, land masses, species, and other subsystems that compose it.

Figure 1.1 (in Chapter 1) represents a hierarchy of living subsystems associated with economic activity. Individuals are basic components of business organizations, business organizations are basic components of economies, economies are basic components of societies, and societies are basic components of the Earth. Because of its supranational position, the Earth cannot be defined simply as the sum of the individuals, organizations, economies, and societies that comprise it. Such a definition would imply that the sole purpose of the Earth is to serve the economic needs of its human citizens. Rather, the opposite is true: Long-term human survival depends on the needs of the Earth superseding the needs of any of its subsystems. In Kenneth Boulding's terms (1956, p. 202), the Earth is the "system of systems" where economic activity is concerned.

Gaia: A Metaphor for Future Survival

As mentioned above, living systems are not necessarily living organisms even though they display such characteristics. However, British scientist James Lovelock (1990) proposes in his Gaia theory (named for the Greek goddess of the Earth) that the Earth is actually a living organism. The basic premise of the Gaia theory is that life and its natural environment have coevolved on the planet. Lovelock (1990) says:

> Geologists have tried to persuade us that the Earth is just a ball of rock . . . and that life is merely an accident, a quiet passenger that happens to have hitched a ride on this rock ball. . . . Biologists have been no better. They have asserted that living organisms are so adaptable that they have been fit for any material

> changes . . . in Earth's history. But suppose that the Earth is alive. Then the evolution of organisms and the evolution of rocks need no longer be regarded as separate. . . . Instead, the evolution of the species and the evolution of their environment are tightly coupled together as a single and inseparable process. (pp. 11-12)

Gaia theory creates a vision of the Earth in which the Earth's living organisms continuously interact with their natural environment to regulate chemical, atmospheric, and climatic processes in much the same way that an organism regulates its internal state. Lovelock's research indicates that the key to achieving the proper environmental balance is species diversity, because diversity helps regulate the climate. As diversity declines, the fluctuations in the weather become more severe. This implies that any massive perturbation within the environment, such as clearing a rain forest, will significantly disturb the Earth's ability to regulate itself (Lovelock, 1990).

Gaia theory has also been fostered by biologist Lynn Margulis. Whereas Lovelock supports Gaia theory by examining macro processes such as weather, Margulis provides a microbiological perspective. She points out that symbiosis, cooperative relationships between organisms from different species, is a universal phenomenon among the Earth's microbes. Over time, symbiotic relationships evolve to the point that the microbes cannot live alone. They form colonies of microbes, each with different functions, for example, breathing microbes, eating microbes, and so on. These colonies evolve into cells, and those cells evolve into plants and animals. Margulis calls these colonies of microbes the "tissues of Gaia," and she says that they have evolved in order to regulate their natural environment. Like Lovelock, she envisions the planet as a living, breathing organism composed of coevolving biological and physical processes. Her observations have convinced her that microbes not only adapt to their environment, but also modify their environment in order to meet their needs. Life and its environment have evolved as one entity, not as separate entities (Joseph, 1990).

Is Gaia real? Is the planet really a living organism? This question will take years of further scientific debate to answer.

At this stage many scientists support the idea and many do not. It really doesn't matter, though, whether the planet is a living organism or not. Environmental scientist Daniel Chiras (1991) says that Gaia theory "is an elegant metaphor that underscores a key principle of ecology: that all living things operate together" (Gallery 1). It is a metaphor that can help humans to better understand their place in the overall ecological scheme. It brings the phrase, "system of systems," to life. If the Earth is perceived as a living, breathing, evolving being that exists through a beautiful and intricate dance of forests, rivers, oceans, atmosphere, microbes, plants, and animals, then people's perspectives on human activities would likely change. Lovelock (1990) says, "In Gaia we are just another species. . . . Our future depends much more upon a right relationship with Gaia than with the never-ending drama of human interest" (p. 14).

Factors of Production: A Living-Systems Perspective

According to the current economic paradigm, the factors of production (land, labor, capital, and entrepreneurial activity) are at the heart of all business activity. Essentially, economic growth occurs when entrepreneurial activity is applied in order to efficiently and effectively organize the other three factors of production in ways that bring the idea to fruition with reasonable financial returns. (Entrepreneurial activity is defined as individuals having an idea as to how to earn a profit and taking the necessary financial risks in order to implement that idea.) Because entrepreneurial activity requires control of the other factors of production in order to implement new ideas, it by definition occupies a superior position among the factors. Further, because the primary goal of entrepreneurial activity is profit, the worth of the factors of production tends to be measured solely in financial terms.

From a living-systems perspective, there are some problems with how the factors of production are viewed within the current economic paradigm. First, in keeping with the idea that the Earth's subsystems should support rather than supersede one another, it should be assumed that the financial goals of entrepreneurial activity need to be compatible with (rather than superior to) the goals of labor and land. If this assumption is made, then entrepreneurial activity would more likely be carried out in ways that are in keeping with the long-term viability of the planet. Note that the authors are not suggesting that entrepreneurial activity is inherently destructive to the environment. On the contrary, as we will discuss in the final part of the book, the ideas produced via entrepreneurial activity could be the seeds of many new methods for ensuring the future survival of the planet while maintaining a viable economic system. The point here is that when entrepreneurial activity is assumed to be superior to the land on which it occurs as well as to the employees who carry it out, there is greater potential for both the Earth and the employees to suffer.

Second, from a living-systems perspective, there is a potential problem associated with using money as the only means for expressing the value of land and labor. The abstract, nonliving nature of money renders it void of the ethics needed to account for living systems. Valuation based solely on money improperly equates human assets and land with the other nonliving assets of the firm, such as buildings and equipment. This exposes the land to the potential for undue exploitation and makes people potentially vulnerable to corporate actions taken purely for financial gain.

Events at the Sperry Corporation's Bristol, Tennessee, plant reveal what can happen when strategic decision makers view their employees and their land in purely financial terms and assume that entrepreneurial activity is superior to these other factors of production. When Burroughs and Sperry merged to form Unisys, executives announced unequivocally that Sperry's Bristol plant, which employed 1,600 workers at the time, would definitely remain open because it was profitable. Two weeks later these same executives announced that they had decided to close the plant for financial reasons; they never disputed the fact that the plant was profitable, but they indicated that closing it would allow them to increase profits by consolidating the plant's functions with Burroughs. In addition, the firm had been illegally dumping toxic wastes on its property for years in order to avoid expensive disposal costs; these wastes were discovered leaching into the area's water supply after the plant was closed. The property has been rendered useless, and no other firms have been willing to buy the plant because of the toxic waste problems; further, many of the former Sperry employees are still out of work or have taken lesser-paying jobs. Were the financial gains achieved by illegally dumping toxic wastes on the land and putting people out of work (even though the plant was profitable) really worth it? Viewing the Earth as a living system might have given the strategic managers at Unisys a different perspective on their decisions.

A number of environmental scientists and economists have suggested that land could be more easily accounted for in living-systems terms if energy rather than money was used to express its value. H. T. Odum (1983) says that using energy to determine land value would allow humankind to account for land in terms of its potential to provide energy on a sustainable basis; this would encourage economic decisions that are compatible with the Earth's long-term survival. Herman Daly and John Cobb (1989) agree, saying that land "is itself an embodiment of solar energy and transforms that energy into the vast multiplicity of living things that make it up" (p. 259).

"Bioregionalism" is another concept that has emerged as a way to place the economic development of land into a living-systems perspective. Bioregionalists advocate dividing the land into natural regions based on native vegetation, geology, and distinctive life forms. These bioregions would develop their economic systems around their regional resources and would be responsible for processing their own wastes in ways most suited to the unique characteristics of that region. This self-reliance would encourage regions to promote economic systems geared toward long-term ecological sustainability (Sale, 1985).

Although somewhat idealistic in today's world of nation-states, bioregionalism offers an enlightening vision of how localities can take a living-systems approach to their economic activities. In fact, the idea has begun to take root in a limited way in the United States. "Think globally, Act locally" bumper stickers abound. States and communities are beginning to act on their own to stop the environmental degradation of their regions. For example, Alabama and South Carolina, states with huge toxic waste disposal industries, have begun to balk at accepting more. The governors of Tennessee and North Carolina shouted at and threatened one another over the dumping of dioxin into the Pigeon River by Champion Paper Company's Canton, North Carolina, plant: The river flows through several Tennessee communities that have recorded extremely high cancer rates and birth defects. Other states have passed laws restricting the production and transportation of toxic substances within their borders, and chambers of commerce and industrial development boards are now beginning to recruit "clean industries." Also, community action groups of every political, religious, and economic ilk are attempting to block firms that are perceived to be an environmental threat from locating in their areas. These activities indicate that people are starting to realize that the land is more than a factor of production: It is the foundation of the living community. As such, it is worth a great deal more than the economic activity it can generate for a few years.

Thermodynamics and Economic Activity

Survival of living systems is based on their ability to exchange energy, wastes, and information with their environment. It is a process of constantly swimming upstream against time, seeking order in a sea of chaos. This process is subject to the laws of thermodynamics, a set of principles governing the movement and transformation of energy in the universe (Ehrlich, Ehrlich, & Holdren, 1977).

That's All There Is: The Conservation Law

The first law of thermodynamics, the conservation law, says that the amount of energy in the universe is constant. Energy cannot be created or destroyed; it can only be transformed from one state to another. Initially, energy is in a potential, "stored" form. This stored energy can be transformed in order to do "work." For example, automobiles burn gasoline (stored energy) in order to transport people (work). The amount of stored energy available for work is dependent on the temperature difference between its stored state and its work state (hence the term, thermodynamics). The greater the temperature difference, the faster the energy flows, and the more "power" it has available to perform work. The smaller the temperature difference, the slower the energy flows, and the less "power" it has available to do work. When there is no temperature difference, the energy is said to be "bound" (unavailable to do work). Gasoline burns at high temperatures and therefore powers a car very well. Water doesn't burn at all, therefore it would be useless to power a car (Ehrlich, Ehrlich, & Holdren, 1977; Odum, 1983).

It Won't Last Forever: The Entropy Law

So, because energy cannot be lost, it will always be here for people to use, right? Wrong. The second law of thermodynamics says that every time energy is transformed from one state to another, some of its available energy to do work is lost. This process is called "entropy." Entropy occurs when stored energy becomes cooler, less concentrated, and/or less ordered when it is applied to do work. When energy is no longer available to do work, when it has degraded to the point of being useless, it becomes a waste product. For example, if you move hot water from the water heater to the wash basin in order to wash the dishes, the heat will escape from the basin into the air, and, as it escapes, the heat will become much less concentrated and less useful for washing the dishes; the water vapor that escapes is wasted energy. Also, entropy is associated with the forward movement of time; things always get older, never younger.

Living systems have the potential for "negative entropy," meaning they can slow down, arrest, or reverse the entropic process temporarily. Life has become more ordered and complex since appearing on Earth as single-celled sea creatures. Living organisms can postpone death by taking in energy from food, water, and sunlight. Organizations can concentrate the ideas and efforts of individuals into powerful, goal-directed entities. However, negative entropy for the living system is not free. It can be maintained only if certain conditions are present: (a) Living systems need a continuous energy source to power their battle against time; (b) they need sufficient information from their environment that they can interpret correctly; and (c) they need sufficient ability to respond to the environmental changes they sense (the more severe the changes, the more complex the response processes need to be).

Whereas entropy is a certainty for the Earth, there is little certainty about the path or time it will take (Georgescu-Roegen, 1971). It depends on how efficiently humankind uses its available energy and how well it responds to the changes in its environment. The Earth and its living subsystems *can* survive and increase in orderliness (as long as there is power from the sun) if people respond correctly to the signals from the environment. Global warming, ozone depletion, acid rain, smog, cancer, energy crises, and ecoterrorism are just a few signals pointing to the fact that changes need to be made as to how humans interact with the planet. The more serious these problems get, the more difficult they will be to control. However, if people respond correctly, the species can survive and develop for a long time to come.

Entropy and the Economy

Because economic activity occurs on Earth, it is subject to the entropy law. Nicholas Georgescu-Roegen (1971) contends that because the entropy law is a natural law that clearly defines the physical limits of economic activity, it should form the foundation on which economic theories are based. He says that the only way to account for the true value of natural resources, the intrinsic value of life, and the actual cost of pollution and overpopulation is to begin basing economic theories on the entropy law. Expanding on this point, physicist Fritjof Capra (1983) says that the mechanical economic models of the past century dismiss the ecological contexts in which economic activity occur.

This leads to a social science that is unable to deal with the dynamics of the natural environment. Assuming that economic activity is not subject to the entropy law leads directly to the fallacious assumption that unlimited economic expansion is possible. He says that "it should be abundantly clear by now that unlimited expansion in a finite environment can lead only to disaster" (p. 213).

Basically, an economy functions by using energy to convert materials from their natural state into usable products or services for consumption by humans. There are three inputs necessary for economic activity: (a) matter inputs (raw materials), (b) energy inputs (the solar flow and terrestrial energy stocks used to power the transformation of matter into products), and (c) information inputs (the knowledge, values, and motives that humans use to determine what to produce, what to buy, etc.) Because energy provides the power for economic activity, the interactions among these three variables are governed by the entropy law.

Whereas the energy used in economic activity is by definition subject to the entropy law, the other two factors (raw materials and information) are not necessarily entropic. Theoretically, matter can be completely recycled; this means that the balance of raw materials needed to maintain economic activity can be maintained indefinitely. Further, information can increase (display negative entropy) in free societies that emphasize relevant education (Boulding, 1966). Thus it is possible in democratic, capitalistic economies to increase valuable information, that is, to learn new values and new technologies; these new technologies can then be used to achieve an economy based on total materials recycling. The only catch is that all of this costs energy. This suggests a basic rule: Conserve first, recycle second, throw away third. If strategic managers can learn to apply this dictum, they will be able to embody the entropy law in their decisions, accounting more completely for the Earth's limits. (We will discuss ways to apply this rule later in this chapter and in Chapter 9.)

Energy and Industry

Most of the Earth's energy comes either directly or indirectly from the sun. The vast majority of the sun's energy arrives directly as sunlight; an average year of direct solar energy amounts to 15,000 times the total world energy supply from all other sources. The sun is also the ultimate source of both renewable energy from wind, hydropower, and biomass, and, nonrenewable, terrestrial energy from oil, coal, and natural gas. Other available forms of energy include nuclear energy (which appeared in the universe before the solar system evolved), geothermal (from the heat inside the Earth's core), and tidal energy (Davis, 1990). Currently, more than 85% of the energy used in the United States comes from oil, coal, and natural gas. About 7% comes from nuclear power, and 7.5% comes from renewable sources (Union of Concerned Scientists, 1990).

Energy and the Economic Cycle

Energy drives the economic cycle. The economy can only operate if there is energy available to power the work of producing and consuming goods and services. Energy use in the economy has risen dramatically during the industrial age. In 1860, the world used the energy equivalent of 10 million barrels of oil per day. Today that figure exceeds 150 million barrels (Davis, 1990).

Money and energy flow in opposite directions through the economy. For example, the farmer's money goes to town in exchange for the fertilizer he needs to power his crops; the manufacturer's money goes to the utility company in exchange for the power she needs to produce her products. However, although money stays within the economic system, energy often exists outside the system. The sun, nonrenewable resources, and other sources of energy that power the economy do not enter the economic cycle until they are purchased and/or converted to fuel. Further, the wastes that occur as a result of converting energy into economic wealth are also considered external to the system. Of course, all economies operate on the principle of balance. Balance of payments, debits equal credits, and costs equal benefits are all basic to successful economies. Unfortunately, because energy sources and wastes are considered external to the economic system, achieving a sustainable balance with respect to energy use and waste generation is not considered important within most economic models that managers apply to their strategic decisions (Odum & Odum, 1976).

This is a significant problem because economic activity requires that energy be converted from a low entropy state (entropy that occurs at slow evolutionary rates in nature) to a high entropy state (entropy that occurs at very rapid rates in production processes) as vast amounts of it are applied to the production of a never-ending stream of consumer products and services (Boulding, 1966; Georgescu-Roegen, 1971). Production-consumption cycles are the primary reason for terrestrial energy sources being used at a rate 100,000 times greater than they are being created in nature. Further, if the projections are correct, energy requirements will increase 50 to 60 percent in the next 20 years because of increasing population and economic activity (Davis, 1990). Therefore, efforts toward preservation, conservation, recycling, and so on need to focus on the processes of producing and consuming goods and services.

Industrial Metabolism

One of the most enlightening frameworks for understanding the environmental impacts of the rapid use of energy employed by humankind's pursuit of economic well-being is "industrial metabolism." Just as living organisms have metabolic processes for transforming the energy they import from their environment into life maintaining processes, economies can also be viewed as metabolic because they extract large quantities of energy-rich matter from the environment and transform it into products for consumption (Ayres, 1989).

Whereas the metabolic processes necessary to maintain life in the ecosystem are balanced and self-sustaining, metabolism in the economic system is grossly out of balance with its environment. The U.S. economy uses approximately seven and a half tons of nonrenewable resources per person each year to produce goods and services. Only 6% of these resources remains in the system for any length of time (basically as durable goods). The remaining 94% of these materials are used to produce food, fuel, and disposable products (e.g., bottles, cans, batteries, and light bulbs) that pass very rapidly through the economic system of extraction to production to consumption to wastes. These wastes are often toxic and harmful to the natural environment. The amount of wastes from economic activities is greater than the combined tonnage of all the crops, timber, fuels, and minerals that remain in the economic system. According to Robert Ayres (1989), these wastes "tend to disappear from the market domain, where everything has a price, but not from the real world in which the economic system is embedded" (p. 27). The damage is done not within the economic system per se, but in the atmosphere, water, and gene pool, which have no current economic value.

Where within this metabolic process does the energy transformed for economic wealth become the wastes that pollute the environment? Of course, the answer is at all points—extraction, production, and consumption. However, most of the loss occurs at the point of consumption. Ayres (1989) says that whereas industry does a very efficient job of acquiring and transforming resources into goods and services, consumption is "naturally dissipative" (p. 26). Most foods, fuels, paper, lubricants, solvents, fertilizers, pesticides, cosmetics, pharmaceuticals, and toxic heavy metals are discarded as waste after a single use, as are thousands of other products. Many of these products are very difficult and expensive to recycle, so not only do people use too many of them, but also they are not likely to use them again.

Toward a Sustainable Energy Flow in the Economy

The basic message of the industrial metabolism framework is that the metabolic processes in the economy need to achieve the same type of balance possible in the ecosystem, when it is absent of economic activity. Just as the ecosystem can sustain itself indefinitely by importing sunlight and using that to power a system that operates almost totally by recycling materials, economic systems must also incorporate sustainable energy in their transformation processes. Special attention should be paid to patterns of consumption because most loss occurs at that point in the system (Ayres, 1989).

Thus one step that can be taken to reduce energy use is to focus on the consumption end of the metabolic process. This can be accomplished in several ways, such as reducing packaging materials, increasing recycling efforts, improving insulation technology, shifting to organic farming methods, and producing high quality, durable products. Because people spend so much nonrenewable fossil fuel just getting from place to place, transportation is a particularly rich arena for reducing the energy consumed. For example, by increasing gas milage to 45 miles per gallon in cars and 35 miles per gallon in small trucks (targets already met or exceeded by several models), 2.8 million barrels of oil a day could be saved. This is more than the United States currently acquires from the Middle East and the Alaskan pipeline combined. Improved public transportation and better energy planning in communities would also help to reduce the energy used for transportation (Davis, 1990; Positive energy, 1991). Electricity use is another rich source of potential consumer energy savings. According to energy expert Amory Lovins (1989), research director of the Rocky Mountain Institute, methods (such as energy efficient appliances and fluorescent lighting) already exist that could help reduce electricity consumption as much as 75% from current levels. However, he is discouraged because so much energy is consumed when the technology already exists to significantly reduce consumption without changing the quality of life. He says:

> The good news is . . . the energy problem has already been solved by new technologies—primarily for more efficient end-use. . . . The bad news, however, is that most governments and private

> sector actors are less committed to market outcomes in energy policy. (pp. 1-2)

Another step that can be taken to achieve a sustainable energy balance in the economy is to change the mix of sources from which energy is derived. Holdren (1990) points out that humankind is neither running out of energy, nor running out of technologies to reduce energy consumption: It is running out of "cheap oil and natural gas . . . , the environmental capacity to burn coal, and public tolerance for the risks of nuclear fission" (p. 157). Humankind can go a long way toward energy sustainability if it increases its reliance on more abundant, more available, renewable, and less polluting energy sources such as the sun, wind, water, biomass, and geothermal. Hydropower (an indirect solar energy source) already provides a significant amount of energy, and wind farms (Don Quixote's dream) are also beginning to appear. Of course, direct sunlight is the most abundant source of potential energy.

Regardless of how promising the renewable energy sources are, the transition to them will be neither easy nor cheap (Holdren, 1990). It will require an investment in improved storage technologies for solar and wind generated power, improved solar electric generating technologies, improved wind turbines, and improved liquid fuels (made from such things as corn and other biomass), among other things. However, if the initial investments necessary for the transition to more sustainable energy sources are made, they could be economically competitive with nonrenewable sources by early in the next century if not before (Weinberg & Williams, 1990). Further, this transition will significantly reduce pollution, environmental degradation, and the political upheaval associated with scarce, unevenly distributed fossil fuels (Fulkerson, Judkins, & Sanghvi, 1990; Holdren, 1990).

In addition to reducing energy consumption and making the transition to renewable sources, society can also continue to focus its attention on energy efficiency in manufacturing. Twenty percent of the world's energy is consumed in industrial processes, and there is a great deal of room for reducing energy loss. For example, 65% of the energy in coal goes up in smoke when it is converted to electricity; a much better efficiency ratio is possible (Ross & Steinmeyer, 1990).

Recycling is one of the most productive ways to increase energy efficiency in industry because it eliminates the most energy-intensive manufacturing steps. It normally requires only about half the energy to produce products from recycled materials as it does from virgin materials. A good job is currently being done in recycling the scrap materials that occur within production processes (Ross & Steinmeyer, 1990). For example, 47% of the iron and steel scrap, 55% of the lead scrap, 40% of the copper scrap, and 46% of the nickel scrap are currently being recycled within industrial processes (Herman, Ardekani, & Ausubel, 1989). However, industry could do a much better job of importing recycled materials from outside the organization to be used in product production; for example, only 20% of the glass, paper, and metal products produced in the United States are made from recycled materials, although 50% is possible (Ross & Steinmeyer, 1990).

Energy efficiency can also be improved through quality control. It is always cheaper to make something right the first time; energy savings are a significant by-product of improved quality (Ross & Steinmeyer, 1990). Another method that can be used to reduce energy consumption in industry is "dematerialization." Dematerialization involves reducing the weight of end products. By reducing the amount of material that goes into a product, the amount of energy it takes to produce the product, transport the product, and power the product is reduced. Dematerialization can also reduce the amount of wastes generated in the production and consumption of a product. Today's cars are a prime example of dematerialization at work. Automobile companies are constantly trying to reduce the weight of their vehicles in order to improve energy efficiency and reduce production costs (Herman, Ardekani, & Ausubel, 1989).

Conclusions

Management happens on Earth. As a living system, the Earth can survive if it maintains a sustainable balance of energy inputs and wastes. The energy-intensive, waste generating economic activities of the past two centuries have seriously destabilized this balance. Energy and materials are being used faster than they can be replenished, and mountains of waste (often toxic) are being created in the process.

Much less energy and materials can be used to satisfy humankind's reasonable economic desires. Recycling, dematerialization, reduced packaging, and so on, can be accomplished. More fuel efficient transportation systems can be developed; food can be grown organically; and low-energy lighting, machinery, and appliances are available. Higher quality products that are more durable can be produced, and a more sustainable mix of energy sources can be developed. Many of these steps will pay economic dividends in the short run, and all of them are economically feasible in the long run. However, changing society's economic behaviors is not going to be easy. Successfully factoring a sustainable balance of energy inputs and waste outputs into managerial decisions will require the adoption of new values that are consistent with sustaining the Earth.

Chapter 4

We Are What We Value

When executives at Quality Devices, Inc. (a manufacturer of kitchen utensils designed to appeal to gourmet cooks) decided to purchase Mountain Empire Furniture Company (MEF) in 1984, it seemed like a great opportunity. The Rocky Top, Tennessee, company produced fine wood furniture designed for trendy urban condominiums; this seemed like a "can't miss" proposition for Quality Devices. The urban professionals buying the condos were also the ones getting into gourmet cooking. This synergy between the two lines of business provided MEF with an excellent opportunity to diversify concentrically. Given the soaring urban real estate market and the seemingly insatiable material tastes of the growing yuppie population, the exorbitant debt the firm assumed when it purchased MEF (financed with high-interest junk bonds) seemed well worth the risks.

Business at Mountain Empire Furniture was great through much of the 1980s. The executives used the money to expand MEF's product lines and to increase the output of existing products, extending its debt even further. Then things began to change. The real estate market went into a deep recession nationwide (nearly a depression in many of the urban areas in which MEF sold a high percentage of its products). Scandals on Wall Street, the collapse of the savings and loan industry, and the paring of middle management layers by organizations in restructuring efforts made many people begin to question seriously their free-spending, materialistic lifestyles. Socially conscious consumers began to balk at buying products that damaged the environment, including those made from tropical or old-growth wood such as that used by MEF in several of its products. MEF was still earning a profit, but servicing the firm's large debt kept it well below what the executives would have liked.

In the past month, workers in the plant began complaining about respiratory problems that they said resulted from breathing the fumes from the laminating and finishing processes. Because of these complaints, MEF hired an independent environmental consultant to audit the firm's compliance with Occupational Safety and Health Administration (OSHA) and the Environmental Protection Agency (EPA) regulations (although they had been inspected only once in their 8 years of operation). The consultant reported that the levels of toxic fumes in the plant would probably meet minimal government standards. However, he also told them that a recent study indicated that exposure to the levels present in the MEF plant over long periods of time might increase workers' risks of contracting lung cancer and other respiratory diseases, especially for those who smoked. More disturbing, however, was the consultant's discovery that MEF's previous owners had illegally buried at least 50 barrels of toxic chemicals in a dump on the firm's property 10 years before Quality Devices bought it.

Sitting around a mahogany conference table, seven MEF executives discuss these issues. What will they decide to do?

In this fictitious scenario,[1] the managers at Mountain Empire Furniture Company are faced with several strategic decisions that have both environmental and economic implications. Will they change the types of wood the firm uses in its products, or will they continue using wood from endangered forests? Will they invest in equipment to reduce the exposure of workers to toxic fumes (and/or invest in an employee smoking cessation program), or will they wait because the firm is probably within minimal legal compliance and is rarely inspected? Will they report the illegal dump and begin cleaning it up, or will they ignore it because the authorities don't know about it and may never find out? How will they balance these environmental issues with the firm's financial goals and obligations and the demands caused by changing market conditions?

Perceptions, Values, and Strategic Decision Making

There has been a dramatic paradigm shift in science during the 20th century. Theories of relativity and quantum physics have led scientists to understand that there is no such thing as objective reality; there are only perceptions of reality. Quantum physicist Sir Arthur Eddington once commented, "The frank realization that physical science is concerned with a world of shadows is one of the most significant of recent advances" (as quoted in Wilber, 1985, p. 9). Werner Heisenberg (1985a), also a quantum physicist, agreed, saying, "Understanding can never mean more than the perception of connections" (p. 56).

This new scientific paradigm has crept into management thought over the past two decades. Perceptual explanations of why and how individuals and organizations behave as they do, explanations that focus on the relationship between people's perceptions and actions, have begun to revolutionize the way many management scholars think about the way decisions in organizations are made.

Perceptions and Organizational Behavior

During much of this century, theories of why people behave the way they do have focused primarily on the environment (Luthans & Kreitner, 1985). These approaches advocate the idea that behavior is entirely shaped by the influence of environmental stimuli and reinforcement. Research on these models has been quite fruitful. However, even in the face of this considerable evidence, scholars and practitioners alike have resisted the idea that humans are primarily motivated by rewards and punishments. Such theories leave little or no room for the influence of human thought processes, the very characteristic that separates humans from other species. Presently, a large body of cross-cultural research has emerged that refutes the idea that humans behave primarily for hedonistic reasons. This research suggests that perceptions play a primary role in human behavior (Ravlin & Meglino, 1987).

To understand the role that perceptions play in human behavior, it is important to realize that people do not operate directly on objective reality. Instead, they operate on their *perceptions* of objective reality. That is, people scan their environment and create a mental picture of that environment; this mental picture involves applying values, opinions, attitudes, beliefs, and knowledge to what is observed and developing a perception of the situation from this process. Once perceptions are formed, people make their behavioral decisions based on these perceptions. Thus humans employ cognitive processes (mental processes involved in having and arranging thoughts) in order to understand and respond to given situations.

Perceptions are formed via a process called categorization (Ilgen & Feldman, 1983; Rosch & Lloyd, 1978). Categorization is essentially a process of reducing information from the environment and storing it in mental categories. Categories are like mental compartments used to store a variety of information that relate in some way. People categorize information from their environment in two ways. Sometimes categorization is automatic, occuring instantaneously for very familiar, overlearned information. Obvious characteristics such as color, sex, and dress are examples of the types of signals that people are likely to automatically categorize. However, people use a more thoughtful, controlled categorization process when dealing with problematic, novel, or unexpected information. Controlled categorization is complex; it requires individuals to pay close attention to information, to consciously search their memory for the appropriate categories needed to interpret the information, and to make conscious decisions about that information

(Ilgen & Feldman, 1983). In fact, actual perception involves both automatic and controlled categorization processes in varying degrees, depending on the situation.

Further, developing perceptions involves both logical, rational, conscious processes, and unconscious, often nonrational processes (Gioia, 1986). Cognitive processing likely begins at the unconscious level, and most of what is processed probably remains at that level. Trying to consciously process all the information received from the environment would be overwhelming and incoherent. Cognitive psychologist Bernard Baars, in his book *A Cognitive Theory of Consciousness,* employs an excellent analogy to explain how unconscious and conscious processes interact to form conscious perceptions. He uses a large number of experts in an auditorium (each with his or her own unique knowledge) to represent mental categories. The auditorium includes a blackboard, which in the analogy represents conscious thought. Just as human conscious thought has limits, so the blackboard has a limited capacity to hold information; it can accommodate only a minute fraction of the information of the many experts in the auditorium. When the experts are faced with a problem, each one searches his or her own memory for information relevant to the problem. The experts who believe that they have relevant information then need to find allies and face conflicts among the other experts in the auditorium; this is the only way that they can register their information on the limited blackboard space and have it applied to the problem. Thus conscious perceptions result from a multitude of unconscious processes that involve both competition and cooperation among the many categories of information available (Harman, 1990/1991).

If people's experiences were always the same, then individuals would likely develop neat categories that could be called upon individually as needed. However, human experiences normally differ from previous ones, requiring people to integrate their mental categories in a wide variety of often unique and complex ways in order to develop meaningful perceptions of their various situations. The term *cognitive map* refers to the integrative mental processes people use when they are faced with behavioral choices; cognitive maps are networks of interconnected mental categories that interact in order to provide meaning and direction for the individual. Cognitive maps are used to translate experiences into knowledge and action, just as road maps are used to explore the alternative routes people may want to take on a trip (Weick & Bougon, 1986).

Of course, people are the basic elements forming the nucleus of all organizations. Therefore, because human behavior is guided by perceptions, organizations can exist only when their members share certain perceptions: They must perceive that they have common goals, they must perceive that there are common methods for goal accomplishment, and they must have a common perception of the organizational members' roles (Weick & Bougon, 1986). In other words, organizations can exist only when the members share a common cognitive framework (Finney & Mitroff, 1986). Thus organizations are often referred to as cognitive networks, "networks of intersubjectively shared meanings that are sustained through the development and use of a common language and everyday social interactions" (Walsh & Ungson, 1991, p. 60).

The popular term used to refer to organizations as cognitive networks is organizational culture (Finney & Mitroff, 1986). Shared motives, shared experiences, shared visions, shared language, shared myths, and shared values all portray the cultural characteristics of organizations. With emphasis on the word *shared*, these terms demonstrate the true cognitive nature of organizations. Shared values deserve special attention here because they dominate organizational decisions that concern which goals are to be accomplished and what criteria are to be used in measuring goal accomplishment (Liedtka, 1989).

Values and Complex Decision Making

One of the most common behaviors humans engage in is decision making; people are faced with making choices all the time. Some choices are based on data that people have access to directly; these choices require little more than an instantaneous, automatic response. A red traffic signal usually elicits an instantaneous decision to move one's foot from the accelerator to the brake. The traffic light and other data (such as other cars or pedestrians) are immediately observable, and the response is automatic, requiring little conscious thought. Other decisions are quite complex. All the data needed are not directly available, meaning that individuals must search their memory for knowledge and metaphors and then consciously process the information available in order to make their choice. Buying a new car is an example of such a decision. Even after all the information is available (prices, options, performance data, etc.), the choice is a nebulous one at best. The dissonance people feel when they make major decisions of this sort is caused primarily by the uncertainties surrounding the decision-making situation.

Managers in business organizations are paid to make decisions, and the majority of decisions managers make are not automatic. Just as buying a car, managerial decisions generally require extensive use of conscious, controlled cognitive processes. For example, decisions about the performance of employees (a standard managerial task) are normally made on the basis of limited opportunities observing the employees at work. These decisions require managers to search their memories for information that may be up to a year old (Ilgen & Feldman, 1983). Moving up the organizational hierarchy means facing more problematic issues that require managers to make decisions with increasingly significant consequences.

Values play a major role in complex managerial decisions (Rokeach, 1968; Yankelovich, 1981). Values are enduring, emotionally charged abstractions (categories) about matters that are important to individuals (Williams, 1960). Understanding values is no simple matter. Some have conceptualized values as existing in hierarchies; that is, some values are always more important to individuals than others. Others say that the importance of any individual value varies. They say that the real key to understanding how important values are in influencing decisions is to discern how important an individual's total system of values is to him or her. This approach views values from a holistic perspective in which the values people favor are influenced by the situation (Ravlin & Meglino, 1987). When people actually apply their values to their decisions, both of these frameworks are likely to come into play to one degree or another. No doubt, some values are more important to people than other values; yet at the same time, the total strength of people's value systems and the situations in which they find themselves are also important.

Social values seem to have a particularly strong influence on the complex choices that individuals make. Social values represent a broad array of behavioral norms, which are best defined by their "oughtness." Social values deal with the way people believe they should behave. Although social values may descend originally from pain and pleasure experiences, they become the social canons of a group, company, community, or society. As such, they serve to control and protect the behavior of individual citizens. This systemic support for social values gives them an existence well beyond any individual reward or punishment. Because social values are expected within the larger group, behaving in accordance with these values is usually endorsed by all members. This is a very powerful motivational force (Ravlin & Meglino, 1987).

People seem to go through a fairly distinctive cognitive process when making complex decisions. They search the characteristics of their situation, determine the consequences of those characteristics, and determine the desirability or undesirability of those consequences (Gutman, 1982). Cognitive choice processes involve choosing (consciously and unconsciously) what information to pay attention to; encoding, storing, and retrieving this information; and integrating the retrieved information into a final choice or decision (Denisi, Cafferty, & Meglino, 1984). Values prove to have an especially strong influence on this process at two points. First, values are critical in helping people determine which elements of their environment are important to pay attention to in making decisions. Second, values are the primary criteria used when choosing among the available alternatives (Howard, 1977; Rosenberg, 1956). The more complex, ambiguous, and subjective a decision is, the more prominent the role of values becomes in the final choice (Jolly, Reynolds, & Slocum, 1988; Reynolds & Jamieson, 1984).

Strategic Decisions: Complex, Value-Laden Choices

Strategic decisions are at the pinnacle of complex choices faced by business managers. Typically, these decisions are made in the upper echelons of the organizational ladder, and their consequences are potentially vital to organizational success. Further, successfully implementing strategic decisions rests on effectively integrating them into the culture of the organization. The complexity of strategic decisions is revealed in the fact that management scholars are not all too clear about what strategy really means. Dozens of definitions exist ranging from the concrete (i.e., Alfred Chandler's determining goals, developing processes, and committing resources) to the transcendental (i.e., Henry Mintzberg's patterns in streams of decisions) (Schwenk, 1988).

What is known is that strategic decisions are ill-structured, nonroutine, complex, and important to the firm (Schwenk, 1988). Further, strategic decisions tend to be unique from situation to situation and from organization to organization. They require managers to have diverse capabilities and relationships, and they require managers to integrate a variety of elements including multiple goals, multiple stakeholders, multiple decision makers, and vague time horizons (Grammas, 1985; Schwenk, 1988; Steiner, Miner, & Gray, 1986). All of this complexity means that the strategic choices made by executives are highly subjective and, as such, are both guided and limited by values (Christensen, Andrews, Bower, Hamermesh, & Porter, 1987; Hambrick & Mason, 1984; Schwenk, 1988). Making strategic decisions in business organizations requires what Gioia (1986) calls the "art of management . . . , the intuitive, insightful, perceptive, nonrational, and holistic [processes] increasingly recognized as characteristic of the complete executive" (p. 339).

The controlled cognitive processes involved in making strategic decisions have been the subject of several writers, one of whom is Charles Schwenk (1984, 1988). He says that strategic decisions are made by invoking a variety of cognitive simplification processes such as ignoring or misinterpreting data that do not fit the decision maker's beliefs, anchoring final decisions on initial value judgments, and using analogies and images to identify problems and solutions. He also says that understanding the strategic decision-making process requires understanding its underlying assumptions. This means understanding the cognitive maps of those executives who make the decisions, because these maps represent the mental structures through which strategic choices are filtered. These cognitive maps provide a clearer picture of current and future strategic choices in the organization.

Finney and Mitroff (1986) discuss how strategic decisions are integrated into the culture of the organization. If a firm wants to successfully implement its strategies, an organizational consensus concerning cognitive schema (mental frameworks that employees use to interpret information) and cognitive scripts (expected behaviors or sequences of events for certain situations) is necessary. Without such a consensus, the organizational culture will not form around accomplishing organizational goals. Further, if an organization can understand its schema and scripts, it may better comprehend how to integrate new (and previously disregarded) information into its existing culture.

Of course, the complex, novel, subjective nature of cognitive processes means that values will be critical factors to both shaping and limiting the final choices made by strategic managers (Schwenk, 1988). Values influence strategic decision makers either directly, by serving as guides to specific action (behavior channeling), or indirectly, by serving as screening mechanisms through which information and alternatives are filtered (perceptual screening). Perceptual screening is considered the more important of these two for strategic decision making because it is the primary way that people apply their values to ambiguous, open-ended, multifaceted situations (Hambrick & Brandon, 1987).

In a recent interview, Robert Haas, CEO of Levi Strauss, provided a practical explanation of why values and the cognitive nature of strategic decision making are so important for managers. He said:

> What we've learned [at Levi Strauss] is that the soft stuff and the hard stuff are becoming increasingly intertwined. A company's

> values—what it stands for, what its people believe in—are crucial to its competitive success. Indeed, values drive the business. . . . In a more dynamic business environment, the controls have to be conceptual. . . . Values provide a common language for aligning a company's leadership and its people. . . . We have redefined our business strategy to focus on core products, and we have articulated the values that the company stands for—what we call our Aspirations. We've shaped our business around this strategy and these values, and people have started marching behind this new banner. (Howard, 1990, p. 134)

Valuing the Commons in Strategic Decisions

This brings us back to the case of Mountain Empire Furniture Company. The strategic choices faced by MEF executives are complex, multifaceted, and uncertain. They are faced with a multiplicity of strategic choices, each with a potential for significant economic and environmental impacts. As was discussed above, what they decide depends on the values the executives apply when they scan their environment and make their choices. Specifically, the decisions made by MEF executives will depend on the strength of their values concerning environmental protection and worker safety.

Without knowing these executives, it would be hard to predict the decisions they might make. Currently, the strategic decision-making deck seems stacked against the environment. We discussed in Chapter 3 that the value of the commons (air, water, and resources everyone needs for survival) is not adequately accounted for in current economic models; this means that MEF executives must go beyond traditional business wisdom if they want to factor the environment more completely into their decisions.

As has been discussed in this chapter, the models that managers use to make complex strategic decisions are the result of cognitive processes whereby the managers apply their knowledge and values in order to develop their perceptions of reality and to determine the direction they will take in dealing with their environment. Why don't today's economic models adequately value the ecosystem? At the heart of the matter may be the insufficiency of current cognitive processes to account for the long-term, seemingly gradual changes that characterize most environmental problems (Ornstein & Ehrlich, 1990).

Most of the man-made changes in the environment have occurred during the industrial age, but the biological evolution of the human was essentially complete thousands of years before. The mental pictures that our ancestors used to comprehend their environment were developed in a very different kind of world than the one that exists today. People lived in small groups in limited, stable, harsh environments. Most of their responses were geared to dramatic, short-term environmental changes. Thus humans developed cognitive models that focused on the short-term. Long-term thinking for our ancestors was season to season; survival was based on their responses to events that occurred daily or moment to moment. They probably perceived gradual global patterns, but had to suppress these perceptions in order to focus on their immediate situations. For most of human history, these short-term mental processes were adequate for survival. The planet was not overpopulated, and there was safety in numbers. People had neither the potential to create long-term global changes nor the ability to deal with these changes when they occurred (Ornstein & Ehrlich, 1990).

Whereas most species evolve only biologically, human beings also evolve culturally. Even though human biological evolution has occurred very slowly, cultural rates of development have been nothing short of phenomenal, especially during the industrial age. The human species went from the horse and buggy to the moon in three-quarters of a century. Humans now have the ability to create long-term global changes. Unfortunately, human perceptual processes are still tied to the old world of short-term, dramatic change; people still suppress long-term perceptual processes to a great extent. Thus perceiving the impacts of the global changes that are occurring is difficult. Humankind continues to reproduce rapidly even though it knows that overpopulation is one of the most serious long-term problems; humans continue to use resources and pollute at incredible rates even though they know that there will be dire long-term consequences. As Ornstein and Ehrlich (1990) say:

> There is now a mismatch between the human mind and the world people inhabit. . . . We are out of joint with the times, our times. . . . The same mental routines that originally signaled abrupt physical changes in the old world are now pressed into service to perceive and decide about unprecedented dangers in the new. . . . The human predicament requires [that we] detect threats that materialize not in instants but in years or decades. We need to develop "slow reflexes" to supplement the quick ones. We need to replace our old minds with new ones. (pp. 10-12)

Ornstein and Ehrlich (1990) contend that people need to take advantage of the flexibility and trainability of the human mind in order to achieve the necessary changes to their mental pictures of reality. Humans are the most adaptable of the species, and they have the potential to synthesize large amounts of information. Education about the problems faced by humankind is important, but education about the way people think may be even more important. If people could learn how they learn, if they could understand how their perceptions influence their view of the world and their reactions to it, then they would be better equipped to modify their cognitive structures to fit the demands of their current environment. Changing cognitive structures, of course, means changing values. Milbrath (1989) says, "We learn and relearn our values. If our lives are not working well, or if society is not working well, we get the message that we need to rethink our value structure" (p. 67).

In order to effectively respond to environmental issues, the strategic decision makers of Mountain Empire Furniture Company will need to develop a mental picture equipped with the necessary values to deal with the long-term implications of these issues. If they perceive the relationship between preserving the rain forests and perpetuating millions of species, if they perceive how long contaminated groundwater takes to cleanse itself, if they perceive how long cancer takes to manifest itself, then the strategic decisions they make will likely reflect the values that emerge from these perceptions. Unfortunately, they may still be operating with the old world mental models that do not give sufficient value to the environment.

Conclusions

Relativity and quantum theory have vanquished the idea that everything from the structure of the universe to the behavior of human beings is a mechanical process governed by deterministic laws. People can only view their world through their perceptions. Perceptions result from complex mental processes that involve applying values to environmental elements. Thus, to a large extent, values structure the mental pictures that, in turn, determine what individuals pay attention to and what actions they take.

Adequately including the ecosystem into the mental pictures that managers use in making strategic decisions can only be achieved by refocusing their perceptions on gradual, long-term processes. Accomplishing this will require changing the way managers are educated. Where should this process start? Where are new models needed most desperately? There is really no choice but to begin with the professed mother of all managerial disciplines—economics. Economic models impart the basic values on which all business choices are based. Thus changing these models is a necessary first step toward more ecologically sensitive strategic decision making.

Note

1. There are hundreds of furniture manufacturers in the small mountain communities of northeast Tennessee that specialize in producing fine wood products. Many are old and have poor ventilation. Because of their number and relatively small size, these firms are seldom inspected by government agencies that are responsible for employee and environmental protection. In 1990 it was discovered that East Tennessee Chair Co., located in Carter County, Tennessee, had been illegally dumping toxic chemicals on its property for years. The dump has since been classified as a State Superfund site.

Chapter 5

Economics As If the Planet Mattered

E. F. Schumacher (1979) often told a story about an economist who, while strolling through the park one Sunday afternoon, came face-to-face with the Lord. The economist was understandably frightened by this encounter and became completely speechless. However, after the Lord assured the economist that He was not going to take him to heaven, the economist regained his composure and decided to ask the Lord a question.

> "When I was a child," said the economist, "the priests always told us that a thousand years on Earth was only a minute to you. Is that so?"
>
> "Yes, that is so," responded the Lord.

Gaining some more confidence, the economist decided to ask another question.

> "If a thousand years for us is but a minute to you, then it must also be true that a million dollars to us is but a penny to you. Am I correct about this?"
>
> "You are correct," responded the Lord, patiently.

Now the economist got very bold. He saw this as his big chance for instant economic wealth.

He said, "Well then, Lord, because you plan to leave me on this Earth for a while, would you be so kind as to give me one of your pennies?"

"No problem," said the Lord. "I'd be happy to oblige you. Unfortunately, I have no pennies with me right now, but if you will wait just a minute I'll get one for you."

Just as there are major discrepancies between the perceptions of the Lord and the perceptions of the economist, there are major discrepancies between the assumptions of current economic theory and the preservation of the ecosystem, the happiness of the planet's human inhabitants, and the dynamics of the global marketplace. As Peter Drucker (1980) points out, there is a crisis in economic theory today because of the "failure of the basic assumptions of the paradigm" (p. 9). He says, "Reality and the available economic theories have been moving further and further apart" (Drucker, 1989, p. 160). Economist Herman Daly (1977) says that applying the assumptions of modern economics is like "seeking the optimal arrangement of deck chairs on the Titanic" (p. 89).

Current Economic Assumptions: Shoes That Don't Fit

In addition to Drucker and Daly, several other scholars have criticized the assumptions of modern economic theory, addressing a broad spectrum of concerns that ranges from the role of the individual and the firm to the true nature of international trade, to the relationship between the economy and the ecosystem. In short, just as children outgrow their shoes, the realities of the marketplace have outgrown economic theory.

Economic Growth: Pie-in-the-Sky Gluttony

As we discussed in detail in Chapters 2 and 3, the assumption that the economy can grow forever is having major negative ramifications on the health of the ecosystem. The environmental costs of this assumption include the rapid depletion of nonrenewable energy, the depletion of natural resources, and the pollution of the natural environment.

Microeconomic theory teaches that organizations should strive to maintain an optimal size determined by several external factors (capital intensity, proximity to customers, etc.). Managers know that striving to have the biggest organization possible regardless of the realities of the business environment is not rational; they know that beyond some size the costs will be greater than the earned income. Yet the idea of optimal size is somehow lost in the shift to macroeconomic theories of the total economy, in which it is assumed that the benefits of growth will outweigh the costs of growth regardless of how big the economy gets.

One way that many economists circumvent the reality that there are limits to growth is by assuming that new technologies will continually appear to counteract the ecological problems. For example, they may assume that less intrusive oil drilling methods will be developed that will allow oil exploration in wilderness areas with less environmental impact, or they may assume that cleaner ways to mine and burn coal will be developed that will allow its continued use as a primary energy source. As Daly (1977) says, "Technology is the rock upon which the growthmen built their church" (p. 105). Although technological innovations (such as the efficient collection and storage of solar energy, cleaner and more efficient production processes, and nuclear fusion) certainly need to be pursued because they offer the promise of helping to reduce the Earth's environmental problems, it cannot be expected that technologies will automatically appear that will neutralize all of the negative impacts of economic growth. Indeed, technology can often cause as many problems as it alleviates. For example, nuclear energy was considered the salvation from fossil fuel dependence in the 1950s, but, in the 40 years since then, no technology has emerged to safely and effectively dispose of the high-level wastes from the process and none seems forthcoming. As Daly and Cobb (1989) say, "The assumption that new technologies will solve the problem . . . does not hold up" (p. 311).

Given the seriousness of our current environmental problems, it seems time to discard the unlimited growth assumption in favor of a more realistic model of the macroeconomy, one that recognizes that the total size of the economy has limits defined by the ecosystem. Again quoting Peter Drucker (1989):

> The final new reality in the world economy is the emergence of the transnational ecology. Concern for the ecology, the endangered habitat of the human race, will increasingly have to be built into economic policy. . . . We still talk of "environmental protection" as if it were protection of something that is outside of, and separate from, man. But what is endangered are the survival needs of the human race. (p. 133)

Ignoring Natural Capital: An Ecological and Social Nightmare

We have argued in previous chapters that the assumption of unlimited growth can exist only if the value of the Earth's natural capital is ignored. One dimension of this problem not yet discussed is the fact that some of the most devastating social and ecological effects of dismissing the value of natural resources are occurring in the Third World. The industrial nations seldom have all the natural resources they need to fuel their economic machines. Japan, for example, has almost no resources of its own, and the European Community is not much better-off. Even resource-rich America imports large quantities of oil, platinum, and other resources from abroad. A high percentage of these resources are imported from Third World nations who often have an abundance of natural capital but few financial resources. Under the current economic system, the rational thing for cash-rich industrial nations to do is purchase their natural resources from cash-poor Third World countries.

However, this solution is flawed for two reasons. First, the resources being traded by these Third World nations are, for the most part, limited and nonrenewable. Because current economic systems have no provision for the loss of natural resources, Third World nations unwittingly transfer huge amounts of their nonrenewable wealth to industrialized nations in return for financial capital. Economist Robert Repetto of the World Resources Institute says, "A country could exhaust its mineral resources, cut down its forests, erode its soils, pollute its aquifers, and hunt its wildlife and fisheries to extinction, but measured income would not be affected as these assets disappeared" (Hinrichsen, 1991, p. 3). Of course, these countries can collect cash only as long as the resources last; once they are gone, there are no other sources of income, and the land is usually left scarred and devastated. This is precisely what is happening to rain forests all over the world. Brazil, Malaysia, and other nations with significant amounts of rain forests are cutting them down and shipping them to Japan, Europe, and the United States for money that will dry up when the forests are gone.

Second, the cash that is paid for these resources seldom adds much to the social welfare of citizens of Third World nations. The resources are normally owned by a few landowners who become wealthy themselves, but who often invest little of that money back into the local or national economies. The jobs that result from trading nonrenewable resources for cash are typically low paying, and the returns on their investment are normally below average (Porter, 1990). New firms in the Third World are normally tied to the excavation or harvesting of resources and, thus, will disappear when the resources are depleted. Economist James Robertson (1990) sums up this problem: "In recent years the world economy has devastated the lives of millions of innocent people, it has been transferring resources systematically from poor countries to rich countries, and it is destroying the Earth" (p. 68).

Human Beings: Selfish Profit Maximizers

One of the economic assumptions most often criticized concerns the relationship between self-interest and the common good. In current economic theory, self-interest is assumed to be the "invisible hand" that guides the market system most efficiently and effectively toward a fair allocation of resources. Extreme individualism is supported because, in theory, maximizing individual wealth is the most direct route to maximizing the welfare of society. Individuals are depicted as self-contained entities who have no need to consider anything beyond themselves when making their choices. Further, it is assumed that individuals are essentially value neutral; they are perceived as having no values except those that can be expressed monetarily. In economic models, humans are similar to the lemmings described in Chapter 1: They are satisfied only when they are consuming.

In his classes at Louisiana State University, Herman Daly used to say that the extreme individualism embedded in current economic assumptions acts as an "invisible foot that kicks the heck out of the common good" because morality, quality time, meaningful relationships with others, and spiritual enlightenment play no part in the model. As Daly and Cobb (1989) say, the radical individualism of current economic theory "excludes concerns for other people's satisfaction and sufferings that do not express themselves as one's market activity. . . . [It] knows neither benevolence nor malevolence, only indifference" (p. 86). Etzioni (1988) agrees, saying, "There is more to life than a quest to maximize one's own satisfaction" (p. 13). He says that morality that evolves from the greater community is as important as individual pleasure in guiding human behavior.

International Trade: Vanilla Theories in a Banana Split World

We discussed previously that ignoring the value of natural capital creates a devastating distortion in the trade relationships between developed and underdeveloped nations. Other economic assumptions of international trade have been criticized as well. Michael Porter (1990) points out that the current theory of comparative economic advantage among nations assumes that capital and labor cannot cross international boundaries, technologies everywhere are identical, products are undifferentiated, no economies of scale exist, and the pool of factors of production in a nation is fixed. The absurdity of these assumptions renders the theory of comparative advantage virtually useless as a tool for understanding international trade.

Porter says, "It is not surprising that most managers exposed to the theory find that it assumes away what they find to be most important and provides little guidance for appropriate company strategy" (p. 13).

Peter Drucker (1989) says that the transnational world economy is, for all practical purposes, ignored in current economic theory even though it obviously influences and sometimes even controls national economic activity. Economic theories have been developed within closed national markets and then fallaciously applied to the international marketplace. To exemplify his point, Drucker uses President Reagan's decision to raise the value of the dollar in the early 1980s. Rather than taking this as an opportunity to sell their products for less in order to protect their international market shares, most American exporters raised their prices to compensate for the money they would lose due to the revalued greenback. In the short-term, they were able to protect their dollar profits, but the higher prices eventually led to decreasing sales as the world market adjusted to the higher valued dollar; within 2 years they were experiencing profit losses. Four years later, the yen went up in value just as the dollar had. In contrast to the American response, the Japanese sacrificed short-term profits in order to maintain market share; their sales did not go down (they actually rose), and their long-term profits increased.

Why Don't the Shoes Fit?
Misplaced Concreteness

Alfred Korzybski (1933) stated years ago that "the map is not the territory." He counseled that it is not wise to confuse signs, symbols, models, and language with the reality they represent. Our languages and our models are mere abstractions of reality, therefore they can never be completely accurate in expressing all the intricate dimensions of what they are meant to describe. All complex subjects require that abstract models be developed which simplify them; understanding requires breaking down a subject into elementary parts that can be examined. No science, physical or social, can evolve in any way other than through the careful development of abstract models that explain the basic elements of the processes involved.

Economics is a highly abstract social science that attempts to explain an incredibly complex subject—how all of the 5.2 billion people in the world tend to behave as they go about satisfying their economic needs and wants. Drucker (1989) believes that economics is already so complex that managers usually cannot develop a meaningful working knowledge of it. Much criticism is leveled at economics because it omits so many important factors, yet everyone agrees that it cannot possibly include everything.

However, the crisis in economics is related not so much to its complexity and abstraction as to the failure of economists to recognize this characteristic. Very abstract and incomplete economic concepts are often presented as if they were complete representations of reality. This problem has been exacerbated by a number of factors, including the current isolation of economics into an academic discipline and the strict adherence to the scientific method in economics (Daly & Cobb, 1989). (Economists such as Adam Smith operated in an interdisciplinary world in which few distinctions among disciplines were made, whereas the scientific method is reductionist by nature, making it difficult to apply to broad, holistic situations.) This problem is known as "misplaced concreteness" (Whitehead, 1925), which means confusing abstract conceptual measures with the reality they are designed to describe—confusing the map with the territory. As Kenneth Boulding (1970) said, "The danger of measures is that they become ideals" (p. 157).

We have already alluded to several of the problems concerning misplaced concreteness in economics. The dogmatic assumptions that individuals are nothing but money-motivated consumers with no moral fiber, that international trade is played on a vanilla playing field, and that natural resources only have value when they are mined or chopped down have all led to major economic, social, and ecological problems. However, we would like to focus particular attention on two outcomes of misplaced concreteness: the misuse of the Gross National Product (GNP), and extreme egoism.

GNP: Misplaced and Misunderstood

Assuming that the economy had unlimited resources and the environmental capacity to grow indefinitely was a rational and harmless simplification of reality when the field of economics was emerging in the 1700s and 1800s. At that time, only a few nations were involved in significant economic activity, newly discovered natural resources seemed endless, and the population was much smaller. Over time, however, economists transformed unlimited growth from a once harmless assumption into fact. Finally, in 1929 a statistical standard called the Gross National Product (GNP) emerged as an official measure of economic growth (Boulding, 1970). Since then, the GNP has become the primary indicator by which societies measure the human welfare of nations; efforts to show significant increases in the GNP drive virtually every monetary and fiscal action taken by the political and economic machinery. Prevailing economic thought says that increasing the GNP is the primary mechanism necessary for achieving prosperity for all the world's people.

However, the GNP simultaneously includes in its measurement of total economic activity a great deal that, in reality, detracts from national prosperity; while at the same time, it leaves out many factors that actually contribute to national well-being. Although some of the money that changes hands within the economy results in healthier and happier human beings, not every dollar is spent to improve human welfare. In a typical industrial cycle, scarce resources are converted into products; the products are then sold, consumed, and discarded as waste. Money is spent throughout this process for a variety of things. The customers, employees, and firms will be temporarily, even permanently, better-off because of the money they receive; however, money is also spent to deplete scarce resources, pollute the environment, and dispose of wastes: All are added into the GNP. In the GNP, depletion and pollution costs are masked as income, and everyone is presumed to be better-off because of it. Thus every time organizations have to drill deeper or invade more wilderness to acquire resources, and every time they dump wastes in a landfill, in the air, or in the waterways, GNP goes up. The $2 billion that it cost to clean up the Exxon Valdez oil spill actually added to the GNP of the United States (Postel, 1990). Daly (1977) says, "We take real costs . . . of protecting ourselves from the unwanted side effects of production and add these expenditures to GNP rather than subtract them. We count real costs as benefits" (p. 99).

Why is GNP so unrelentingly worshiped in economics? The belief that increasing GNP and improving human welfare go hand-in-hand has persisted despite overwhelming evidence that the economy cannot grow big enough or fast enough to benefit the majority of the world's exponentially growing population, and, if it did, the ecosystem could not absorb the stress. Boulding (1970) says, "The GNP is like the Red Queen in *Alice Through the Looking Glass*: It runs as fast as it can to stay where it is" (p. 158). Unfortunately, as long as unlimited growth is assumed to be a reality rather than a simplifying assumption, GNP will be synonymous with human welfare. Schumacher (1979) is quite graphic about this point:

> How can anybody assert that growth is [always] a good thing? If my children grow, this is a very good thing; if I should suddenly start growing, it would be a disaster. . . . Therefore, the qualitative discrimination is the main thing; it's far more important than some mysterious adding-up of everything. (p. 125)

Egoism: Individualism Gone Wild

Etzioni (1988) points out that exchanges seldom occur among equals; usually one party has a power advantage over the other. This means that powerful individuals, firms, unions, or special interest groups can often dominate the free market. American business has indeed been rocked many times in the past decade by powerful executives and organizations who decided that their primary goal was to serve their personal interests, implementing what Freeman and Gilbert (1988) call managerial prerogative strategies (such as golden parachutes, poison pills, and leveraged buy-outs). This is another example of misplaced concreteness; the assumption that economic activity is based on the self-interests of moral-free individuals looking for financial gain has been confused with more complex social realities.

Examples of egoistic practices abound. In 1986 Frank Lorenzo bought Eastern Airlines for $620 million ($280 million of that was his own cash). He bled Eastern Airlines dry while infusing capital into Texas Air, which he also owned. Eastern was saddled with $500 million in new debt, stripped of its assets, and eventually bankrupted. Many people lost their jobs, but Lorenzo cleared $200 million (Gibney, 1989). Donald Kelley, CEO of Beatrice, was paid $6.75 million for helping structure the Beatrice leveraged buy-out. Then, as chairman of BCI Holdings Corporation (the company that resulted from the leveraged buy-out), he was paid $13 million in salary and received another $227 million as profit. All of this occurred within 2 years (Levitt, 1987). Donald Trump and Robert Campeau are other names often associated with egoistic business practices. However, the most blatant example of egoism in business may be Charles Keating, former CEO of Lincoln Savings and Loan of California; during his tenure, Lincoln Savings and Loan lost $2.6 billion of its depositors' money in the junk bond market. At one of the court hearings concerning possible fraudulent practices by Keating, an internal memo from Keating to his junk bond salespeople was presented as evidence. It read, "Always remember, the weak, meek, and ignorant are always good targets" (Martz, 1990, p. 22).

Debate over egoism in the United States has been fueled recently by reports of the excessive compensation received by many executives. *Business Week, Industry Week,* and *Newsweek* are but a few of the national publications that have focused on high executive pay. Even *Forbes,* the business magazine that has most glorified high executive pay over the years, published a scathing cover story in 1991 about firms that have compensated their CEOs excessively. In 1990 a CEO's salary in a midsized firm in the United States averaged a hefty $2.1 million, and the pay for executives in large firms averaged $3.3 million (Nelson-Horchler, 1991). Further, the pay gap between executives and workers in the United States widened tremendously in the 1980s;

executive salaries rose 212% during that time, four times faster than the average worker's salary (Thomas & Reibstein, 1991). The highest CEO salaries in the United States were below $1 million in 1980; they are now approaching $35 million (Thomas, 1991). CEOs in the United States earn between 95 and 150 times as much as the average production worker. This is much greater than the pay differences in either Japan or Germany (the ratio in Japan is about 15 to 1 and in Germany it's about 20 to 1), yet many feel that these countries have gained significant competitive advantages over the United States in the past 10 years (Nelson-Horchler, 1991).

Two factors seem to have contributed to the growing shareholder, employee, and consumer outrage over excessive executive compensation. First, CEOs are given their raises by boards of directors who, for the most part, are handpicked by the CEO; CEOs even serve on each others' boards, leading to the appearance (if not the reality) that they have vested interests in scratching each others' backs (Thomas & Reibstein, 1991). Second, many of the exorbitant increases occurred despite poor performance by the firm; they have come at times when stock values and profits had dropped, or when the firms were facilitating budget cuts, wage freezes, and layoffs of middle and lower level employees (Nelson-Horchler, 1991).

One of the most publicized cases of high executive pay during a period of poor company performance occurred at ITT in 1990. The board doubled CEO Rand Araskog's compensation, awarding him a total pay package worth $9.7 million. This was done during a year when ITT's profits plummeted 30%; ITT's earnings per share had dropped in 5 of the previous 9 years prior to Araskog's raise, and its stock has consistently remained a poor performer (Nelson-Horchler, 1991; Thomas, 1991). Another example is CEO Thomas Petry of Eagle-Picher Industries, who was awarded a 38% raise during a year when the firm's profits fell 27% and it filed for Chapter 11 bankruptcy. Also, Stephen Wolf of United Airlines was paid $18.3 million in 1990 while its profits were falling 71% (Thomas & Reibstein, 1991).

Shareholders are beginning to respond directly to such practices. One of the largest investment funds in the nation, the

$60 billion California Public Employees' Retirement System (CalPERS), has openly confronted ITT over Araskog's compensation. CalPERS (which claims to own about one percent of every major firm in the United States) is a major shareholder of ITT. CalPERS General counsel Richard Koppes says, "ITT is one of the worst performing shares in our portfolio. Imagine what Araskog will be worth if ITT does well" (Thomas, 1991, p. 50). Others are taking the same approach as CalPERS has; as large pension funds from New York, Wisconsin, and other states join the fray, proxy battles over excessive executive pay are brewing in all corners of U.S. industry (Thomas & Reibstein, 1991).

New Economic Models

In sum, the current economic paradigm has had a destructive impact on the natural environment, favors egoism over the moral standards of the greater community, has led to incredible abuses of power, and has reduced the ability of the United States to compete in the global marketplace. Drucker (1989) is very pessimistic about the role that economic theory will play in the future. He says, "To give us a functioning economic theory, we need a new synthesis. . . . And if no such synthesis emerges, we may be at the end of economic theory" (p. 157). Economists and noneconomists alike have labored diligently over the past few years to foster new economic theories based on more realistic assumptions about the greater environment in which the economic system is embedded.

Replacing Unlimited Growth With Sustainable Development

More than anyone else, E. F. Schumacher brought the world's attention to the problems of unlimited economic growth. His publication of *Small Is Beautiful* in 1973 was a wake-up call for the world. He said that the first assumption of economics should be that there is such a thing as "enough." Once such an assumption is in place, then economists and other scientists can go about the business of defining what "enough" is (Schumacher,

1973). Herman Daly (1977) proposed that "enoughness" needs to be a primary value on which economic theory is based if humankind is to achieve a sustainable balance between the economic system and the ecosystem.

Enoughness implies that there is a sufficient level of economic consumption beyond which human welfare and ecological balance are significantly eroded. Defining what is sufficient is no easy task because it is an attitude as much as it is a specific amount of goods consumed. However, the results of ignoring sufficiency are a great deal more ominous than assuming that it exists, albeit imprecisely. Daly (1986) says, "Perhaps the only thing more difficult than defining sufficiency is our present attempt to get along without the concept by pretending that there is no limit to either the possibility or desirability of growth" (p. 43).

A primary reason as to why current economic theory does a poor job of dealing with sufficiency is that economics ignores the ultimate ends for humans—purpose, happiness, fulfillment, and enlightenment; and it ignores the ultimate means of achieving these ends—using limited resources and energy (low entropy). Economics is stuck between the two: It focuses only on intermediate ends such as comfort, and intermediate means of achieving these ends such as technological devices and labor. If the ultimate means and ends were a part of the economic paradigm, then humankind would "recognize that the ultimate means are scarce, and that the ultimate end is such that, beyond a certain level, it is not served by further physical production" (Daly, 1977, p. 177).

Including the ultimate means and ends within economic thought would add concrete meaning to the concept of sufficiency. That is, sufficiency would take on more meaning in the economic system if it were assumed that human beings want happiness, fulfillment, enlightenment, and a sense of purpose, not just more things, and if it were assumed that there are only limited amounts of energy and resources available for people to pursue these ends. Both assumptions are critical for a new, ecologically and morally sensitive economic paradigm to emerge. Defining the personal and ecological dimensions of sufficiency provides the opportunity to build an economic paradigm around the idea of sustainable development—healthy economic activity that provides for individual happiness and fulfillment without placing undue stress on the small planet, Earth.

Accounting for Nature

Daly and Cobb (1989) say that the term "land" in economic theory should be renamed "nature." As a factor of production, land is assumed to be lifeless and inert, something that can be bought, traded, sold, and lived on. Thus (as we discussed in Chapter 3) land is considered an almost perfect substitute for money and other forms of capital. However, nature is alive and full of energy. People don't live on nature; they live with it. People may swap land for money, but they can never buy nature.

Achieving sustainable growth requires the development of meaningful economic tools for including the value of nature in economic models. Essentially, these tools should internalize costs that have in the past been considered external to the economic system. This is a particularly sticky problem because many of these external costs are pervasive, going beyond specific resources, organizations, communities, or nations (Daly, 1977). Nonetheless, several attempts have been and are currently being made to bring the external costs of damaging nature into the system.

James Robertson (1990) suggests a three-pronged tax system designed to internalize environmental costs. His first proposal is a land occupation tax based on the site-value of the land (the value of the land prior to any improvements such as buildings). Using the site-value allows the tax to be levied on the value of the property before it enters the traditional economic cycle. Second, he suggests taxing energy and resources before they are mined or harvested, again accounting for their value in nature prior to their entry into the economy. These taxes should be based on the caloric value of the resources (calories are a measure of the potential energy something contains) rather than the dollar value. Third, Robertson would tax pollution and wastes. He acknowledges that implementing pollution and waste taxes will be more difficult than implementing the first two. They will require a plethora of taxes, each focusing on specific waste and pollution problems, for example, garbage taxes, soil erosion taxes, air pollution taxes, water pollution taxes, and so on. "Certainly, it could provide meat and drink for a small army of environmental economists and bureaucrats," he says (p. 108). However, he points out that the complexity of the waste and pollution tax system can be offset at least partially by the energy-resource taxes; these are designed to encourage organizations to be energy and resource efficient, because greater efficiency means less wastes and pollution.

An approach that is currently getting more attention than taxes is the use of market incentives to control environmental problems. Such approaches are designed to reward firms for controlling wastes and pollution before they occur. One approach is to issue pollution credits that allow a firm to emit a certain amount of pollutants into the environment. These credits are tradable assets; that is, companies whose emissions are below that allowed by their credits can sell the excess credits to other firms. For example, the 1990 Clean Air Act has a provision for tradable sulphur dioxide credits (we will discuss this in more depth in Chapter 8). Also, Colorado Senator Tim Wirth has proposed a similar system for tradable carbon dioxide permits. In the summer of 1991 there were more than 100 bills before the U.S. Congress that proposed some type of market incentive as means for controlling environmental problems (Begley & Hager, 1991).

Daly (1977) believes that these market mechanisms (both taxes and market incentives) are good ideas, but he doesn't think they go far enough toward internalizing environmental costs into the economic system. He says that they cannot be counted on to solve all of our ecological ills because they don't directly address the issue of absolute scarcity of our resources. Daly believes that depletion quotas should also be imposed—limits on the absolute amount of resources that can be extracted in a given period of time. Like Robertson's land and energy-resource taxes, depletion quotas would recognize the value of resources in their natural state. Like pollution credits, depletion quotas would be tradable on the open market, providing positive incentives for organizations to save resources. Thus these depletion quotas would provide controls over our scarce resources, yet would maintain a free market system to allocate them.

Because the gross national product is the primary instrument used to measure welfare in society, redefining the GNP is a critical step toward bringing natural environmental costs into the economic system. Daly and Cobb (1989) propose alternative approaches to GNP that better account for the Earth, including one they call Hicksian Income (HI). The concept was named for Sir John Hicks who wrote over 40 years ago that sustainable income was the only kind of income that has any real meaning. Simply stated, when people cannot sustain their income, they become poor. Hicksian Income begins by calculating the net national product (NNP), that is GNP minus standard depreciation costs. Net national product alone is a better measure of sustainable growth than GNP because it recognizes that growth has some costs associated with it—wear and tear, repairs, replacement, and so on. However, it does not include either depreciation of natural capital (DNC) or defensive expenditures (DE), income spent to protect ourselves from the ecological side effects of production, such as money to clean up an oil spill or toxic waste dump. Hicksian Income is thus calculated by subtracting DNC and DE from NNP.

In practice, the job of redefining a nation's GNP to include the natural environment is no simple matter. An ecologically based index must include things for which there are currently no generally accepted measures. Because of these difficulties, no nation, until recently, had made a concerted effort to actually find an ecologically sensitive substitute for the GNP. Germany has now begun a 10-year project to develop a "Gross Ecological Product" that will conform to traditional economic accounting practices, yet take the natural environment into consideration. This is, no doubt, a tremendous undertaking for the 40 statisticians and economists assigned to the project by Germany's Federal Statistical Office. Norway, Sweden, France, the Netherlands, Canada, and Japan are also trying to develop natural resource accounting methods, but their efforts are not as ambitious as the German project (Hinrichsen, 1991).

Replacing Egoistic Lemmings With Moral Human Beings

Amitai Etzioni (1988) proposes that the assumption of radical individualism prevalent in current economics be replaced with what he refers to as the "I/We paradigm." The I/We paradigm recognizes that humans make rational economic choices designed to satisfy their individual needs and desires, but it also recognizes that individual economic satisfaction can only occur within the moral dimensions of a meaningful community structure.

The I/We paradigm makes three assumptions that foster a more realistic perspective of human beings. First, it assumes that people have many needs and wants. In addition to economic desires that can be measured in dollars and cents, people also want to live up to moral values unrelated to the economic system. Second, the I/We paradigm assumes that people typically make their choices on the basis of value judgments and emotions and only secondarily through empirical logic. Third, it assumes that people exist as parts of social collectives that impose moral standards of conduct. Individual relations are largely molded by the community in which they take place. Thus, in the I/We paradigm, humans are perceived to be multi-directed, emotional, value-laden, and unable to function effectively except within acceptable moral limits of the community (Etzioni, 1988).

Daly and Cobb's (1989) "person-in-community paradigm" is similar to the I/We paradigm. They point out that people are both consumers and workers in an economic community in which relationships with one another are important. Further, the economic community is a smaller part of larger social, political, and ecological communities, and, thus, it should serve the moral priorities of these larger communities. Within their paradigm, the foundation unit of the economic system is the self-sufficient community, not the selfish individual.

Daly and Cobb (1989) recommend several steps for implementing the paradigm, including land taxes, resource taxes, waste taxes, and depletion quotas (as discussed earlier), as well as changing the nature of free trade (to be discussed in the next section). Further, they suggest that more political and economic powers be pushed down to the state and local levels; this would encourage people to be more active in democratic processes because it would allow individuals a greater sense of identity with their communities.

Two of their recommendations address the problems associated with extreme egoism. First, they suggest a return to prior governmental policies designed to prevent consolidation of economic power into the hands of a few individuals and organizations; tax and ownership laws should be structured to encourage spin-offs and discourage mergers. Second, they propose that income tax laws be modified so that the income gaps between the rich and the not-rich are less extreme. They clearly state that income differentials are important free market incentives and should not be abandoned; however, extreme income differentials ignore the important interdependencies among members of the community (Daly & Cobb, 1989).

One feature of the person-in-community paradigm that is of particular interest to business managers concerns labor-management relations. Daly and Cobb (1989) say that management and labor constitute a single community of mutual interests. They advocate small employee-owned organizations that are energy-efficient and provide real opportunities for personal employee satisfaction with the work. Such organizations tend to do less environmental damage, foster the group over the individual, and help to restore thought, skill, and initiative to the workplace.

Addressing the Realities of the Global Market

Michael Porter's *The Competitive Advantage of Nations* (1990) is probably the most complete attempt to dislodge the current economic theories of international trade. He proposes that current theories do not even address the right question. Current theories focus on understanding why some nations are more competitive than others, but Porter points out that nations do not compete: Industries and industry segments are the competitors in the global market. For example, Japan is not a competitive nation; it has many competitive industries and many noncompetitive industries. The same is true of Germany, Italy, and the United States. The role of the nation is to serve as the "home base" of the competitors. Thus the proper question is, Why do particular nations provide favorable environmental conditions (a good home base) for the emergence of globally competitive firms and industries?

He dispels many myths about international trade. For example, he points out that many nations are quite well-off despite high trade deficits or high exchange rates for their currencies. He also shows that an abundance of cheap labor or natural resources is usually a poor mechanism for achieving advantages in the global marketplace. The advantages once provided by low wages and cheap natural resources are now being replaced by the ability to adopt new technologies that bypass or reduce dependence on these factors. He says that nations like India and Mexico have built their economies on cheap labor, but they are not exactly ideal industrial role models. He says, "The ability to compete *despite* paying high wages would seem to represent a far more desirable national target" (Porter, 1990, p. 3).

Porter (1990) identifies four determinants of a nation's ability to provide an effective home base for particular firms and industries. First are factor conditions: A nation should be able to adequately create, upgrade, and specialize its human, physical, knowledge, and infrastructure (communications, transportation, etc.) factors to meet the needs of its industries. Of these, the most important are "advanced factors" like sophisticated electronic communication capabilities, highly educated personnel, and a strong commitment to scientific research. The second determinant is the demand conditions that exist within the home base nation. Firms and industries that are required to constantly innovate and improve in order to be competitive at home will typically be better equipped to compete abroad. The third determinant is the presence of strong related and supporting industries (suppliers, software firms to support computer manufacturers, etc.). And the fourth determinant is how well the strategies and structures of the firms within an industry fit the dynamics of the global market, as well as, how much rivalry exists between the firms in an industry.

Porter makes two points about the ecological dimensions of international trade. As mentioned, he warns against basing competitive advantages on cheap natural resources (Porter, 1990); he also argues that strong environmental regulations in home-base nations provide global competitive advantages for firms in industries affected by the regulations (Porter, 1991). He points out that Germany, with the world's strongest environmental laws, supplies 70% of the air-pollution control equipment sold in the United States.

Daly and Cobb (1989) agree with Porter that low wages are not a competitive advantage and that international trade takes place between individual firms and industries rather than between nations. They also agree with Porter that basing trade on cheap natural resources can create problems. They note that massive debts accumulated by Third World nations (e.g., Brazil) have forced them to overharvest rain forests and other natural resources to meet their financial obligations. They say that ecological and social dimensions would be more prominent in international trade if it were conducted between national communities rather than individual firms. Nations could more effectively seek multilateral balances based on the physical amounts of resources traded (as opposed to financial balances). This would allow a nation to have resource deficits or surpluses with specific nations while maintaining an overall balance. Such balances could be achieved by auctioning import quotas to firms in amounts relatively equal to what a nation expects to export in a given period of time; these quotas could be resold or traded to others, but no more quotas would be issued during the trading period. Thus positive incentives are provided to firms, and global natural capital transfers are kept to a sustainable level (Daly & Cobb, 1989).

Conclusions

We began with a story, and we will end with one. A cruise ship sank in a storm several years ago, and one of its rafts was left adrift with three people aboard—a physicist, an engineer, and an economist. The raft was stocked with a survival kit that included canned goods, but the can opener was missing from the kit. The physicist said that this presented a very perplexing problem because they had no way to separate the strong metal molecules of the cans in order to get to the food inside. The engineer agreed, lamenting that there were no sharp instruments on board that they could use to open the cans. The economist, however, dismissed the pessimistic realities of his fellow passengers, saying, "All we have to do is assume that the cans are already open. Then we can eat to our hearts' content."

The fallacious assumptions that frame a great deal of our current economic thought make it extremely difficult to apply traditional economic models with any degree of success. In this chapter, it has been documented that new economic paradigms are springing forth from both inside and outside the discipline of economics. Because strategic managers make the vast majority of their decisions within the global economic system, they are the ones most in need of new paradigms. Concerns for the Earth are now being shouted to business organizations by consumers, investors, and the public-at-large. In order to deal effectively with these concerns, managers are left with no choice but to apply new models, values, and methods. The survival of their firms depends on it.

PART THREE

Managing on a Small Planet

In the previous five chapters we have demonstrated that a change is needed in the way business is practiced, and we have established a conceptual framework for successful economic decision making within the limits of the ecosystem. In this part we present a framework for applying these foundations to strategic decisions made by business managers. We begin by discussing the emerging new management paradigm: We propose that it is necessary to better incorporate the limits of the Earth into this new paradigm. We then suggest a set of values that managers can adopt in order to make their strategic decisions more compatible with the Earth's limits. Next, we discuss pressures from stakeholders, pressures that dictate more environmentally sensitive business activities. Finally, we present the concept of sustainability strategies; that is, business strategies that recognize the interdependence between long-term economic success and environmental sustainability. If managers adopt values compatible with the planet and make their economic decisions within a framework of ecological sustainability, the authors believe that economic prosperity within the limits of the ecosystem is possible over the long run.

Chapter 6

Toward the New Management

The field of management emerged during the second half of the 19th century as industrialization captured the attention of the world. As is true of all the disciplines that emerged during that time, management's beginnings were heavily rooted in the mechanistic model. The mental prototype of the business organization during most of *this* century has been a manufacturing firm with long, impersonal assembly lines stationed by workers performing narrow, mindless tasks, and led by managers relying on formal authority, precise procedures, and unbending rules in directing workers.

Adam Smith shaped the economic thought from which these mechanistic structures appeared. He espoused the concept of division of labor based on the mechanistic view that a person's behavior could be broken down into small, standardized parts. The field of management emerged when Max Weber's bureaucracy and Frederick Taylor's scientific management provided the organizational structure and job engineering techniques necessary to make division of labor an operational concept that could be meaningfully applied in large-scale manufacturing organizations.

Thus, with Taylor and Weber, the mechanistic management paradigm was born. Within this paradigm, organizations are viewed as goal-directed entities made of coordinated parts, those parts being people. The job of the manager is to make these parts work together more efficiently, cutting labor costs and improving profits. Hierarchical authority is bestowed so that knowledgeable managers can give orders and expect compliance. Middle management levels swell as the need to pass information and orders within the hierarchy grows. Workers are seen almost exclusively as means to ends, hired for their hands but not their minds.

The Emerging Management Paradigm

However, as we discussed in Chapter 4, the scientific paradigm has changed. Relativity and quantum physics dispel the belief that the universe is a deterministic machine. A new paradigm has emerged that sees the universe as an interconnected whole. Reality is seen as relative, depending on the perspective of the observer. The management paradigm is adapting to this new worldview. More flexible structures are replacing hierarchies; global mind sets are becoming dominant; and organizations are emerging as interconnected networks of employees, suppliers, and customers that strive for human and social fulfillment as well as economic goal accomplishment.

Seeds of Change

New paradigms do not appear overnight, and the new management paradigm is no different. Although it began taking shape in the 1980s with the publication of such works as Tom Peters and Robert Waterman's *In Search of Excellence* (1982), William Halal's *The New Capitalism* (1986), Peter Drucker's *The Frontiers of Management* (1986), and Gareth Morgan's *Images of Organizations* (1986), it has been emerging for more than 50 years.

Ernest Bader was one of the first executives to practice the new management paradigm. Bader was a British industrialist who founded Scott Bader, Ltd., a plastics manufacturer. He began applying his philosophies of employee welfare, participation, and social responsibility in the 1930s. He described his holistic organizational philosophy in 1945, speaking of the need to view workers as humans rather than as parts in a machine, providing them with meaningful work, respect, and social satisfaction. He said:

> If we had some faith, some inner conviction, about the whole purpose of our working, might that not give a new meaning to the working day? . . . Increases in wages or better conditions of work can be no moral equivalent for pride in craftsmanship, social recognition and acclaim, opportunities for advancement, and the free expression of personality and initiative. (Hoe, 1978, p. 80)

Further, he clearly recognized that business success was dependent on satisfying the often conflicting needs of multiple stakeholders; he believed that employees were the most important stakeholders because others are less committed to and dependent on the organization for survival. Again quoting Bader:

> The classes of persons entitled to their . . . satisfactions are the owners, the customers of the products or services, and the workers. Between these three is a constant jostling. . . . The stake of owners and customers in a business are temporary, transient, and partial, but the employee normally gives all his working time to one business and therefore seeks in and through it a much wider personal satisfaction. (Hoe, 1978, p. 80)

Bader proved his overriding commitment to his employees in 1951, when he gave them the company, making the Scott Bader Commonwealth the first employee-owned company in Britain. This unique organization still operates successfully today. Its operation is based on a code that stresses the organization as a working community; measures success of the organization in terms of technical, social, and political as well as economic dimensions; makes it the expressed duty of managers to make all jobs personally fulfilling for employees; mandates that decisions in the firm be made by consensus; and states that all employees are responsible and accountable for making decisions about their jobs. Further, the code includes commitments to produce only beneficial products, to protect the natural environment, and to question any activity that appears to waste the Earth's resources. With its people-oriented, participative structure, its multiple stakeholder focus, and its acknowledgement that organizations can serve social and ecological as well as economic needs of society, the Scott Bader Commonwealth has a tremendous head start on the 21st-century organization. E. F. Schumacher (1978) once described Ernest Bader as "a tragic figure, because he has as yet had few imitators" (p. xiii). Today it could be said that most organizations in the world want to imitate him.

In the 1940s, 1950s, and 1960s, a number of management scholars began to suspect that organizations were something more than machines for producing and selling goods and services. Kurt Lewin (1947) tied directly the ability of organizations to manage change to effective group dynamics. Chris Argyris (1957) stressed that organizations should be structured to meet the needs of mature adults. Douglas McGregor (1960) stressed worker autonomy and creativity. Rensis Likert (1961) found that participative organizations can achieve greater economic success because of their supportive relationships and ambitious performance goals. Frederick Herzberg (1960) introduced the idea that redesigning jobs to include more growth and development opportunities improves worker motivation and performance.

While these scholars provided clues as to what the new organization might look like, others provided insights as to why these new structures would be necessary in the future. Scholars such as Burns and Stalker (1961), Emery and Trist (1965), and Woodward (1965) demonstrated that increasing environmental turbulence and advancing technological systems would dictate the need for more flexible, dynamic organizational structures that rely on more informal, knowledge-based decision-making processes.

The 1973 Arab oil embargo, an event described by E. F. Schumacher (1979) as the economic watershed of the century, marks the beginning of an extremely turbulent era for business. "Things will never be the same again," he said (p. 5), and they haven't. The embargo provided the small crack that many manufacturers (e.g., Japanese automobile manufacturers) needed to get a stronger foothold in the international market. From that point the global economic race was on. Besides its economic aspects, the embargo exposed the vulnerability of major economic powers to the political actions of small nations. Today the term "environmental shock" (an event that has a strong, immediate effect on economic activity, such as the Gulf War) has become commonplace in business.

This explosion of political turmoil and global business activity following the embargo has been paralleled by incredible advances in technology and the awakening of a social consciousness among people. Information technology and biotechnology have revolutionized the way people process information, the nature of the products produced, and the way products are manufactured (Handy, 1989). The increasing social and environmental demands from citizens have led to unprecedented levels of consumer advocacy, social activism, and legislation aimed at changing the way organizations do business. These complex economic, technological, political, ecological, and social demands are all factors faced by today's business organizations. According to Peters (1990b), "The interaction of volatility, globalization, and information technology is leading to the speedy restructuring of all old industries . . . " (p. 76). In his much acclaimed book, *The Age of Unreason,* Charles Handy says, "We are now entering an Age of Unreason . . . , a time when the only prediction that will hold true is that no predictions will hold true" (p. 5).

Thus it has become apparent that the survival of business organizations in the future will require implementing new organizational structures and management practices never dreamed of by Taylor or Weber. Practitioners and scholars alike have discovered that organizations need to look and act a little more like the Scott Bader Commonwealth, and a little less like the Roman Army. From this, a new management paradigm for the third millennium has begun to emerge.

Dimensions of the New Paradigm

As mentioned earlier, a number of important works have appeared in the past decade that have redefined the practice of management. Tom Peters and Robert Waterman focused the world's attention on the shifting paradigm in 1982, when they published *In Search of Excellence.* Today the new paradigm is taking center stage in the field of management (F. Rose, 1990). For example, Stanford University has recently instituted a course on this new paradigm in its business school, which focuses on business as a path to enlightenment, inner wisdom, and spiritual fulfillment (Stewart, 1991a).

We discussed in Chapter 4 that organizations are now perceived as mental, information-processing networks that function through shared values, shared visions, and shared communication systems. The recognition that they are mental networks rather than physical entities allows organizations to discard their rigid, impenetrable internal and external boundaries in favor of permeable, flexible ones. The discussion below focuses on some of the key dimensions of this emerging organizational framework.

From Machines to Meatballs and Spaghetti

A central theme of the new paradigm is that organizations operating in the current business environment can best survive and prosper if they adopt more organic structures. These structures are as different from their classical, mechanistic counterparts as the name suggests. They are flexible, informal, knowledge-based systems with multidirectional communication channels designed to respond rapidly to changing environmental conditions. Halal (1986) describes an organic organization as "a fluid tangle of individuals and units going their own way in a larger web of societal connections" (p. 151). In trying to picture such an organization, it may help to quote a senior manager of a large, organically structured construction firm. "Most companies are structured like machines," he says. "We are structured like a plate of meatballs and spaghetti, with the meatballs being the people and the spaghetti being the lines of communication." In a recent teleconference, Tom Peters (1990a) gave a similar description, saying that the organization of the 21st century will look like a circle with everyone thrown into the middle of it. Jack Welch, CEO of General Electric, says that one of his goals is to see GE become an organization without boundaries (F. Rose, 1990).

Instead of strict hierarchical control, these structures emphasize information processing and knowledge as the foundations of decision making. As Drucker (1986) points out, the knowledge base in today's organizations has shifted from the top to the bottom. With this shift comes the need to change the role of managers from commanders to information processors. Instead of telling workers what to do and how to do it, managers in organic organizations are responsible for getting the right information to the right place at the right time so that the workers can decide what to do and how to do it themselves.

Organic organizations are participative in nature. Because knowledge is dispersed throughout the organization, organizational members need to develop processes for sharing responsibility and accountability. Halal (1990) says, "Managers and employees are beginning to work together, finally, because it is becoming clear that sharing rights and responsibilities can greatly increase productivity in a more competitive world" (p. 46). He notes that the increase in employee stock ownership plans (ESOPs) provides a striking example of the fact that participative systems are taking hold in business. Ernest Bader began planning to give his company to his employees in 1946 (completing the transaction in 1951), proving again what a visionary he was (Hoe, 1978).

The primary structure for participative decision making in today's organization is the team. The growth of quality teams and product teams in organizations over the past decade is nothing short of phenomenal. Peters and Waterman (1982) popularized the term *skunk works* to describe ad hoc teams that cut across functional lines in order to complete specific projects.

Drucker (1986) believes that such ad hoc structures will replace the permanent department as the foundation unit of the modern organization. These teams normally consist of specialists from a wide variety of functions who apply their varied knowledge to the project at hand. They form around ideas, they stay together until the idea comes to fruition, and then they move on to other teams with other ideas. The organization pushes decision-making authority and responsibility down to these teams. The Tomy Toy Company of Japan, for example, does not place its design engineers, production engineers, and marketing personnel into functional departments. Instead, it simply instructs them that toys are fun. Their job is to have fun designing, producing, and selling them. These specialists form teams that take new concepts for toys from someone's idea through design and production into the marketplace. And Tomy Toy is not unique. IBM, GE, TRW, and Clark Equipment Co. are other examples of companies that are decentralizing, allowing people to choose their own jobs and to start ventures within the firm (Halal, 1986).

Organizations today are creating internal market structures in which teams buy and sell goods and services (internally or externally) and hire the employees they need, bringing the free market system inside the organization (Halal, 1986). Rather than being held responsible for a choking array of rules, regulations, and procedures, the teams are free to operate within broad strategic guidelines, and their performance is determined by how well they accomplish their strategic objectives. These internal free markets organize themselves around the ideas of "intrapreneurs." According to Pinchot (1985), intrapreneurs are people (or groups) who have an idea and are willing to take the risks necessary to see that idea come to fruition. Successful intrapreneuring involves building effective teams around these innovative ideas and crossing organizational boundaries for resources, people, and information.

As authority and responsibility are pushed down to these ad hoc teams, organizations are able to cut multiple layers, thus becoming flatter and having fewer managers. Multiple layers made perfectly good sense when they provided efficient information-processing channels for the limited amounts of information that needed to be transmitted between the higher decision-making levels and the lower production levels. However, they make little sense in today's information-rich environment and its sophisticated electronic processing techniques. Drucker (1988) says that the organization of the next century will have half the layers and one-third the managers as those of the mid-1980s.

The external boundaries of organic organizations seem to almost disappear as well. Organizational relationships with suppliers and customers become cooperative and service-based rather than competitive and cost-based. Peters and Waterman (1982) noted that closeness to the customer is fundamental for doing business, saying, "The excellent companies . . . seem more driven by their direct orientation to their customers than by technology or by a desire to be a low-cost producer" (p. 157). Recently, Peters (1990a) has said that no organizational planning should take place unless customers and suppliers are a part of the process. Modern just-in-time systems eliminate inventory buffers in favor of strong customer-manufacturer-supplier relationships; products are conceived on the basis of customer use rather than only on internal expertise; the manufacturers, the suppliers, and the customers are considered an integrated network of entities with common goals (Stewart, 1991b).

More Is Out, Better and Less Are In

Another dimension of this new management paradigm is the concept of smart growth, discussed most completely by William Halal (1986). He presents convincing arguments that changing economic trends (such as the decline of materialism) and increasing environmental problems are rapidly rendering hard growth (growth achieved via increases in physical commodity production) infeasible. Smart growth involves turning today's economic and environmental problems into tomorrow's business opportunities. Economic growth in the future will occur within organizations and industries that contribute to improving the quality of life. Industries such as day care, waste management, pollution control, educational services, and information processing will likely grow, while basic manufacturing industries will continue to decline. He says:

> Values are changing. . . . People in advanced economies are becoming disenchanted with growth as an end in itself, material consumption is often unsatisfying, many distrust the complexity of technology, and they fear the insidious effects of pollution. Instead, they are becoming interested in social relationships, satisfying jobs, and other aspects of the quality of life. (p. 37)

Halal (1986) contends that the transition from hard growth to smart growth has been a three-decade evolution that began with challenges to unlimited material progress during the student activism of the 1960s, continued during the self-examination and inner-growth period of the 1970s, and was solidified by the hard economic realities of the 1980s. This transition has led to a new, more thoughtful American dream that balances the advantages of economic growth with its social costs. Halal (1986) calls this a transition "from more, to better, to less" (p. 81). Tom Peters (1990b) agrees, saying that the great economies of the world cannot expect to continue to grow through greater commodity production. He says that the "battleground has shifted from more, more, more . . . to better, better, better" (p. 73). Competitive advantage for the business organization of the 21st century is going to be gained through factors such as speed, flexibility, quality, design, skill upgrading, and globalization.

Smart growth is not limited to external strategic processes. It is also a major internal focus of firms as they prepare to do business in the next century. Lean and mean is the term you hear today when executives discuss their internal structures. We already mentioned that organizations are cutting out layers of managers. They are also using computerized production and office automation technology to slice blue collar and clerical jobs. Firms today are focusing on increasing revenues while trimming their workforces. Again, Peters and Waterman (1982) hit the nail on the head when they said, "Small in almost every case is beautiful. . . . Small, quality, excitement, autonomy—and efficiency—are all words that belong on the same side of the coin" (p. 321).

Holistic Thinking Replaces Linear Thinking

The new management paradigm is also characterized by a shift in the way that managers think about the problems they face. According to Senge (1990) the old management paradigm was dominated by linear thought processes that dictated that managers view organizational problems as "cause-effect chains" (p. 73). He says that linear thinking in organizations led to seven organizational "learning disabilities" (p. 21). These include: (a) thinking in terms of individual jobs rather than in terms of the whole organization; (b) blaming problems on people or things that are outside the organization; (c) believing that organizations can always solve their problems by taking aggressive action against whatever external force they believe is causing problems; (d) becoming fixated on specific, sudden events; (e) being unable to perceive threats that result from slow, gradual processes; (f) believing that they immediately experience the consequences of their decisions; and (g) operating under the myth that management teams interact cross-functionally to solve problems when, in reality, these teams often spend tremendous energy defending the self-interests of individual members.

According to Senge (1990), linear thinking should be replaced with holistic, systems thinking that will allow organizations to see the broad, dynamic, recurring processes that underlie organizational problems. He says that systems thinking allows organizations to understand that circular rather than linear relationships are at the heart of most organizational problems. He says, "Reality is made up of circles. . . . In systems thinking it is an axiom that every influence is both cause and effect" (pp. 73, 75). Gareth Morgan (1986) says that once organizations begin to think in terms of "mutual causality" (p. 247) rather than in straight, cause-effect lines, then identifying the true nature of relationships among the key variables of a situation becomes possible. Uncovering these relationships can lead to identifying the underlying patterns that perpetuate the problem over time.

Senge (1990) gives a simple example of how this circular pattern works in business: A company produces a superior product that leads to satisfied customers; the satisfied customers pass the word about the high quality of the product to others; demand for the product then rises; the company produces more products, which leads to more satisfied customers, which leads to more word-of-mouth about the high quality of the product, and so on. In this way, the firm grows rapidly. However, if the firm does not recognize the circular relationships among these variables, then demand could begin to exceed the firm's ability to produce the demanded number of products and still continue to meet its high-quality standards. If this occurs, then the firm may cut corners on quality in order to meet demand, and the cycle will reverse itself. Customers will buy the lower quality products, become dissatisfied, and spread the word that the quality of the product is below par. All of the sudden, sales will begin to fall. The key to avoiding this problem is recognizing the circular, holistic relationships among quality, customer satisfaction, positive image, and sales.

Profits Move From Center Stage

What many believe to be the most significant transition from the old to the new management paradigm is the shifting perspective toward the profit motive. Once considered to be the only purpose of business organizations, profits today are more often considered indicators of how well organizations are serving the needs of their stakeholders—their customers, shareholders, employees, and society at large, all of whom have an interest in the practices of the corporation. This is not to say that profits will soon disappear as an important business variable. But, as Rensis Likert (1961) said 30 years ago, profits do not simply appear, but rather result from good management practices.

Serving the varied, often conflicting, needs of these multiple stakeholders requires the organization to develop multiple goals formulated in social and political as well as economic terms. Because of this need to develop multiple goals for multiple stakeholders, the management focus of organizations has become more strategic (Halal, 1986). Ansoff (1979) says that because the strategic problems facing organizations are being complicated by increasing customer sophistication, expanding global markets, increasing environmental and social awareness, changing technology, and escalating turbulence, management processes in organizations must become more strategically focused. Halal (1986) says that strategically managed organizations are not just companies with strategic plans. These organizations don't just have a strategy: They have a philosophy of creating strategies, adapting to the environment through innovation and entrepreneurial activity.

As mentioned earlier, Ernest Bader took a multiple stakeholder focus almost 50 years ago, and he believed that employees are the most important of a firm's stakeholders. Today this philosophy has been adopted by many organizations. For example, GE's new organizational philosophy focuses on the human being as the key to future productivity (F. Rose, 1990). Indeed, quality of work life has become a primary focus of business organizations all over the world. Freeman and Gilbert (1988) believe individual worth should be the value that forms the foundation of an organization's principles. Their basic premise is that an individual "has the basic right to pursue his or her own projects . . . free from coercion and interference from others. . . . Individuals are ends and never mere means to someone else's ends" (p. 82). They refer to this as a "personal project enterprise strategy." They believe that this philosophy will provide not only fulfillment for employees, but also a more ethical approach to customers and suppliers as well.

Increasing stakeholder awareness and the much publicized greed of the 1980s focused a great deal of public attention on business ethics. Author Thomas Wolfe said, "We are leaving the period of money fever that was the eighties and entering a period of moral fever" (Farnham, 1991). As usual, Wolfe was on target. As the 1980s came to a close, it became clear that unethical business practices were of grave concern to society. Major business publications (*Fortune, Wall Street Journal,* etc.), depicted the business ethics of the 1980s as greedy, selfish distortions of the free enterprise system. Respected organizations such as The Business Roundtable and Touche Ross concluded that ethical behavior in business is one of the most challenging issues facing America in the decades ahead (Stead, Stead, & Worrell, 1990).

Thus ethics became another dimension of the new management paradigm that focused attention away from the profit motive. Cavanagh, Moberg, and Valasquez (1981) espouse that human rights and justice must be as much a part of organizational decision making as utilitarian concerns. Freeman and Gilbert (1988) point out that all business strategies have an ethical foundation regardless of whether management is aware of it. They believe that organizations should apply ethical reasoning to their strategic decision-making processes, analyzing who is affected by the decisions, how they are affected, what rights the parties have, and so on.

All of this leads to the realization that organizations that serve the needs of the greater society in which they exist are more likely to prosper. The narrow economic niche in which business organizations once resided has expanded into a much broader societal niche (Zenisek, 1979). It is generally understood today that social performance cannot be separated from economic performance. As well as earning a profit, organizations today are expected to contribute to social welfare. Halal (1986) says:

> The key to restoring economic vitality today is to recognize that social goals and profit are not only compatible, but so interdependent that the firm cannot succeed unless it unifies these two sets of concerns. (p. 229)

This quote is exemplified by a recent decision in rural Washington County, Virginia. The Virtex Chemical Company purchased 10 acres in an industrial park in the county and applied for a permit to manufacture sodium azide, a chemical used in automobile air bags. Although the county desperately needs economic development (two major employers have recently closed down), the citizens of the county voiced serious concerns about the environmental impacts of a chemical plant being located there. The county commission denied the permit. Virtex was not allowed to locate there because social concerns outweighed economic concerns in the mind of the community. The people were saying, "Meet our social needs as well as our economic needs, or don't come here." (Since its experience in Washington County, Virginia, Virtex has also been denied permits to operate in Carter and Hawkins Counties in Tennessee because of the same environmental concerns.)

Including the Earth in the New Paradigm

The practice of management has, no doubt, expanded beyond its economic roots. The field is currently going through a revolutionary change: paying attention to values, human beings, and the greater society. It is focusing on ethics and social responsibility. It is facing up to the reality that hard growth is not possible forever and has even begun to put profits in their proper perspective. In addition, management scholars are beginning to speak of the need to account for the limits of the planet in managerial practice. Halal (1986) noted that the limits of the natural environment are a major reason why smart growth should replace hard growth as the focus of business strategies. The term itself, smart growth, is quite appealing from an ecological perspective. However, current management theory is still inadequate in accounting for the natural world.

Paul Shrivastava (in press) of Bucknell University has been quite critical of the narrow focus of the term *environment* as it appears in management literature. He says that *environment* as it is currently conceptualized in management focuses almost exclusively on economic and social factors, paying little attention to nature. He uses the conceptualization of "population ecology" theory as one example to support his point. He says that, although population ecology theory and methodology are based in the environmental sciences, the natural environment is not included within the framework of the theory in management.

Earth: The Ultimate Stakeholder

Because the natural environment has not yet achieved its proper place in the management paradigm, strategic decision makers are too often faced with seemingly insolvable conflicts between environmental protection and economic success. They don't necessarily want to ignore the environment, but they have a difficult time putting the environment in its proper perspective. How does a strategic manager weigh the environment? How much consideration does it deserve in relation to the firm's other stakeholders?

The model we presented in Chapter 1 (Figure 1.1) may prove enlightening here. The living Earth is the paramount system, the umbrella under which all the stakeholders of business organizations exist. Societies, communities, suppliers, consumers, shareholders, and organizations themselves are all subsystems of the Earth. Thus logic would suggest that the Earth should be considered the ultimate stakeholder in business organizations. As we have said before, the Earth is the only source of capital for economic activity, and it can produce new capital only at evolutionary speeds. The economic subsystem needs to be geared to the Earthly processes. There really is no choice; the Earth cannot gear itself to the speed of current economic activity. As Jim Post (1991) of Boston University says, "As global natural resources are depleted, the survival potential of the planet is itself at stake. Never before has Earth itself become a stakeholder of such significance to corporations and managerial decision making" (p. 34).

E. F. Schumacher: A Beacon to the Future

E. F. Schumacher was an erudite gentleman who was born in 1911 and died in 1977. He was a brilliant economist who attended Oxford and Columbia. Lord Keynes once deemed him the most worthy candidate to carry the mantle as the world's top economist after his own death. As is true for most people, Schumacher's ideas matured and changed as he matured and changed. He began life as an arrogant, atheistic intellectual who disdained formal education and religion because he believed himself smarter than his teachers and ministers. He focused only on facts, believing that they explained everything. However, as he grew older he turned to Buddhism and eventually Catholicism. As his religious and social enlightenment progressed, his ideas about economic systems became more spiritual than intellectual, and he found that the most important things in life were learned from the common man and from the soil, not from economic experts with all their facts and figures (Wood, 1984).

During his life, he contributed as much to our knowledge of the economic, technological, and agricultural dimensions of a sustainable society as anyone. He said that modern industrial society was living under three dangerous illusions: (a) unlimited growth is possible in a finite world; (b) there are unlimited numbers of people willing to perform mindless work for modest salaries; and (c) science can be used to solve social problems (Schumacher, 1979). To him, these illusions were paths to resource depletion, environmental degradation, worker alienation, and violence. He coined the phrase, "Small is beautiful," and he dedicated his life to seeing the phrase come to reality.

Fritz Schumacher had a great deal to say about management in the future. Like his friend Ernest Bader, Schumacher was writing about and practicing the new management paradigm early on. He provides one of the first complete frameworks for making strategic decisions within the limits of our small planet.

The Theory of Large-Scale Organization

Schumacher (1979) once said, "The time has come to work with the dinosaurs, the large corporations" (p. 74). He believed that large organizations inhibit freedom, creativity, and human dignity. He believed that the only way to reverse this in vast organizations is to "achieve smallness within the large organization" (Schumacher, 1973, p. 242), and that is the premise on which he based the theory of large-scale organization.

The theory consists of five principles. The first says that large organizations should be divided into "quasi-firms," small, autonomous teams designed to foster high levels of entrepreneurial spirit. The second principle says that accountability of the quasi-firms to higher management should be based on a few items related to profitability. Decisions are to be made by team members in ad hoc fashion without interference from upper management; upper management only steps in if the profitability goals are not being met. Third, the quasi-firms should maintain their own economic identity; they should be allowed to have their own names and keep their own records: Their financial performance should not be merged with other units. Fourth, motivation for lower-level workers can be achieved only if the job is intellectually and spiritually fulfilling with ample opportunities to participate in decisions; this can only be achieved in small, meaningful groups. And finally, top management can balance the need for employee freedom with the need for organizational control by setting broad, strategic performance targets and allowing the quasi-firms to make their own decisions within these targets (Schumacher, 1973).

He thought that the structure of a company organized around these principles would resemble a helium balloon vendor at a carnival with a large number of balloons for sale. The vendor (who represents top management) holds the balloons from below rather than lording over them from above. Each balloon represents an autonomous unit that shifts and sways on its own within the limits defined by the vendor. Schumacher said that organizations should be structured "like nature with little cells" (1979, p. 83).

Good Work

Schumacher (1979) said, "Business is not there simply to produce goods, it also produces people" (p. 73). According to Schumacher, organizations have the responsibility to provide "good work" for employees, work that is enjoyable and that satisfies the creative and spiritual needs of employees. Schumacher (1979) was very passionate in his descriptions of good and bad work. He said:

> How do we prepare young people for the future world of work? . . . They should be encouraged to reject meaningless, boring, stultifying, or nerve-racking work in which a man (or woman) is made servant of a machine or a system. They should be taught that work is the joy of life and is needed for our development, but that meaningless work is an abomination. (pp. 118-119)

Schumacher (1979) believed that good work could be found only in organizations that allow human dignity and freedom to flourish in small autonomous groups like those he described in the theory of large-scale organization. He believed that the lack of available good work in our bureaucratized, mass production society was the primary contributor to inflation—when there is no intrinsic fulfillment from the job, the natural tendency is for employees to focus on getting more money for what they do. Further, he believed systems would have to change if the principles of good work were to be successfully adopted into society. He said that education will have to deal more completely with traditional questions such as: What is man? Where does he come from? What is his purpose? Only when people find their own answers to these questions will they be able to identify what type of good work is their path to fulfillment and enlightenment.

Appropriate Technology

In the mid-1950s, while working as an economic advisor to the British National Coal Board, Schumacher came to the conclusion that industrial technology was taking an irreparable toll on the natural environment because of its overuse of fossil fuel energy. In 1954 he warned that our current economic activities were creating dire problems because of technologies that relied on massive amounts of nonrenewable energy resources (Wood, 1984).

Although his warnings fell on deaf ears during the industrial expansion of the 1950s, this realization was a personal breakthrough for Schumacher. From that point on, it was abundantly clear to him that the technologies of the industrial age were built on dreams no more real than puffs of smoke (Wood, 1984). He saw these technologies as being inhuman, favoring the rich over the poor, and destroying the very Earth on which they exist. He realized that if society did not develop technologies that were more sensitive to human and environmental concerns, then our days on this planet were numbered (Schumacher, 1973).

From these concerns, Schumacher (1979) began to develop his ideas of "appropriate technology." (He actually referred to it as intermediate technology.) He based appropriate technology on three assumptions: (a) It is possible to make things smaller; (b) it is possible to do things simpler; and (c) it is possible to do things cheaper. If these assumptions are true, then production technologies can be developed that stress low-cost methods and equipment which are available to most people, can be used on a small scale, and are compatible with man's creative needs. When Schumacher discussed low-cost technologies, he didn't mean just financial costs: He meant total costs, measured in terms of the depletion of the Earth's natural capital as well as the purchasing, operating, and maintenance costs (Schumacher, 1973). He said that technology should be developed which provides for "production that respects ecological principles and strives to work with nature . . . " (Schumacher, 1979, p. 57).

Much of Schumacher's life was devoted to the application of appropriate technology. He formed the Intermediate Technology Group in 1965 (Wood, 1984). This group, which is still quite active, is committed to developing culturally, ecologically, and humanly sensitive technology in the poorer regions of the world (Schumacher, 1979). Schumacher's work with the group took him to India, Zambia, and many other Third World countries in which he applied his ideas to their economic development. Ironically, he probably benefited from these experiences more than the nations he was trying to help. He was exposed to Buddhism and other forms of eastern mysticism in many of the countries where he worked. The ideas of peace, wholeness, and human spiritual fulfillment that he garnered through these experiences are interwoven throughout his later works (Wood, 1984).

Although appropriate technology has been applied primarily in poorer nations, it is also applicable in richer, industrialized nations. As we have already demonstrated, the people of the wealthy nations of the world certainly need more modest, humane, ecologically sustainable economic systems. Appropriate technology provides many important insights into how this might be achieved. As a matter of fact, the book *Good Work* is primarily composed of lectures Schumacher gave in North America shortly before his death that concern the benefits of appropriate technology in highly developed economies (Gillingham, 1979). George McRobie (1979), cofounder, with Schumacher, of the Intermediate Technology Group, says that poorer nations need appropriate technology in order to achieve affordable economic development, but richer nations need it in order to achieve a more sustainable lifestyle.

Scott Bader Revisited

We would like now to return to the Scott Bader Commonwealth. As we mentioned earlier, Ernest Bader and Fritz Schumacher were friends. More than that, their relationship was one of synergy, each becoming a better person as the result of his interactions with the other (Hoe, 1978; Wood, 1984). Schumacher helped Bader arrange for the transfer of the Scott Bader Commonwealth to the employees in 1951. He became a director of the company when the employees took over ownership and remained in that capacity until his death.

He described his experiences with the Commonwealth as among the most meaningful of his career. Practicing what he preached was always of the utmost importance to Schumacher (Gillingham, 1979). His association with the Scott Bader Commonwealth allowed him to apply his ideas about ecology, organization, work, and technology. As an ESOP, it represented the perfect people-oriented, participative organization—ideal for implementing the theory of large-scale organization. Because it manufactured polyesters, it represented a real environmental challenge—ideal for implementing appropriate technology in a developed economy. As a member of the board, he was able to help develop an organizational value system that emphasized smallness, community involvement, and ecological sustainability. The firm set up a parliament of workers with control over the board of directors, limited its growth to 400 employees, refused to sell to armament manufacturers, and earmarked 50% of its profits for philanthropic purposes (Schumacher, 1979).

Schumacher was prophetic when he used the famous phrase, "I have seen the future and it works" (Schumacher, 1979, p. 78) to describe his experiences with the Scott Bader Commonwealth. Today the firm is an excellent example of the new management paradigm at work. It has a flat, participative, organic structure; it has an intense commitment to remaining small, flexible, and smart; it values the spiritual fulfillment of the worker, the good of the community, and the protection of society as paths to earning profits; and it recognizes that the Earth is the ultimate stakeholder. It currently employs about 365 people, attracting employees who seek jobs that do not exploit the environment and that provide them with fulfillment (McMonies, 1985). It continues to successfully blend commercial success with quality of work life and a desire to save the world. Its experience demonstrates clearly that a firm can combine commercial and social values (Bader, 1986).

In discussing the contributions of E. F. Schumacher, economist and futurist Barbara Ward said that he "belongs to that intensely creative minority who have changed the direction of human thought" (McRobie, 1979, p. vii). However, his friend George McRobie (1979) summed up his contributions to the management paradigm of the 21st century best:

> Fritz Schumacher . . . [brought] his personality and creative energy, as well as his remarkable mind, to bear on what is certainly one of the most critical tasks that now confronts rich and poor societies alike: how to enable us to do creative and satisfying work, earn a decent living, live in a becoming way; and having done so, to leave the planet Earth in a condition at least no less capable of supporting life than in which we found it. (p. xi)

Conclusions

As humankind enters the next millennium facing burdensome overpopulation, increasing political turmoil, unprecedented technological innovation, and rapid environmental degradation, a management paradigm is needed that provides organizations with openness, flexibility, quality of work life, social awareness, and ecological sustainability. This paradigm has begun to take shape in the management literature. Organizations are now viewed as organic, holistic, value-driven, quality-driven, information-processing networks with permeable internal and external boundaries. They are lean and mean, smart, and motivated by enlightened self-interest that puts profits in their proper perspective.

The next step is for organizations to fully integrate the Earth into the new paradigm. As a system, the Earth encompasses its subsystems—societies, communities, organizations, consumers, employees, and all individuals. Therefore the Earth is the ultimate stakeholder in business activities. As such, it is necessary that strategic managers adopt values and implement strategies that will allow organizations to achieve long-term economic success within the sustainable limits of the planet. E. F. Schumacher has shown the way. Now managers must follow his lead.

Chapter 7

Values for a Small Planet

As we have demonstrated throughout the book, the viability of the planet is directly threatened by the current levels of economic activity. The long-term sustainability of the economic system is, no doubt, intricately intertwined with humankind's ability to sustain the ecosystem. Further, we have shown that complex strategic decisions made in business organizations are shaped to a great extent by the values held by managers making those choices. We have also presented new paradigms in both economics and management that stress broader human and ecological concerns, and we have demonstrated that firms who adopt these new paradigms can be successful in today's competitive business environment. All of this leads to a central message: Economic success in the 1990s and forward into the 21st century will require organizations to formulate and to implement business strategies that account for the limits of the Earth. The first step toward these environmentally sensitive business strategies is for those managers making strategic decisions to adopt values that integrate economic success and environmental protection. In this chapter, we suggest some values that will make this possible.

The Manager's Divergent Dilemma

Many of the problems humans face are convergent in nature; meaning that if they apply linear thinking to the problem, some type of reasonable answer(s) will emerge eventually. For example, if a group of people want to know how to get from Birmingham, Alabama, to Nashville, Tennessee, data indicate that they will have to travel 190 miles due north. All of the possible solutions available (the roads they can take, the modes of transportation they can use, etc.) must eventually move them that many miles in that direction.

Other problems people face are of a divergent nature. Unlike convergent problems, divergent problems defy solutions attained with linear logic. The more straight-line logic applied to such problems, the more diametrically opposed and outrageous the solutions become. E. F. Schumacher (1977) used a divergent problem faced frequently by business managers to demonstrate this—how to balance freedom and control in organizations. Arguing for freedom, it is certainly well documented that creativity and motivation are best served by a free and open organizational environment that gives all employees the opportunity to excel at whatever they do best. From a linear perspective, if freedom is a good, then more freedom is better, and complete freedom is the best of all. Following this logic to its conclusion leads to an organization characterized by anarchy, chaos, and a total lack of direction.

Therefore, it seems that the solution to this problem lies in exercising control. Control allows for direction, standardized behavior, and more efficient goal accomplishment. Straight-line thinking will lead to the conclusion that if control is good, then more control is better, and total control is best. Of course, following this logic leads to an organization that resembles a prison, one so rigid that independent thought is completely absent among employees (Schumacher, 1977).

As this example illustrates, straight-line logic is inadequate in dealing with divergent problems. Managers are likely to be unhappy with either of the above outcomes; they want neither complete chaos nor total rigidity. Solving this problem requires transcending it—recognizing an underlying structure that rises above these dichotomous solutions. This means identifying a value system that, when applied to decisions concerning freedom and control, will strike a synergistic balance between the two. Schumacher (1973, 1977) said that the key value in this case is respect for the human being; once managers recognize that humans are capable of self-awareness and self-control, balancing freedom and control becomes quite possible. Managers can maintain control by clearly setting broad goals and by espousing the important values of the firm; then, within the boundaries of the organization's goals and value system, employees can be given the freedom to make decisions about how to take the firm where it wants to go. Firms like General Mills, Federal Express, 3M, and Aetna have developed organizations that employ this type of thinking. Essentially, strategic managers in these firms establish broad goals, objectives, and expectations; teams of employees are then set free to develop their own objectives, procedures, and processes within these guidelines (Dumaine, 1990). From a company the authors consult with often, one CEO says, "My employees play the game; my job is to keep them between the goal posts."

We have established throughout the book that managers face a very tricky divergent problem when protecting the natural environment is concerned. How can managers balance economic survival with ecosystem survival? One side of this argument is that economic survival requires economic growth. Economic growth means continued opportunities for the citizens of the planet to improve their quality of life. Applying linear logic to this argument, if economic growth is good, then more growth is better, and so on. Taken to its logical conclusion, it is desirable that economies grow at exponential rates forever, using resources (both natural and human) as nothing more than means to economic ends. However, as we have documented, the environment in general and humankind in particular are suffering already from the results of this flawed linear thought process.

The opposite approach is just as unacceptable: Ecosystem survival certainly requires maintaining and preserving the resources and processes necessary to support life on the planet; therefore, if maintaining the ecosystem is a good thing, then totally closing off the environment to the effects of human economic activity would be the perfectly logical solution to current ecological problems. No economic growth would be permitted; resources would be treated purely as ends and would never be used to serve humankind's needs. This solution would spell total economic collapse, hurtling humankind back into the dark ages. The Earth undeniably has problems now, but the environmental impact of 10 billion people trying to "live off the land" without the efficiency and other benefits of modern economic systems (such as technology, communications, and distribution) would be equally devastating. Ironically, the probable results of this argument would resemble those currently being experienced because of exponential growth: pollution, degradation, species loss, human suffering, violence, and so on.

As was true of the freedom/control dichotomy, the key to solving this dilemma lies in developing a system of values that rises above these arguments. These values would need to transcend these polar opposites. Such a value system would help people understand that economic and ecosystem survival are both worthy and necessary goals for individuals, organizations, societies, and the ecosystem. Such an understanding would allow previously opposing forces (e.g., environmentalists and strategic decision makers in business organizations) to recognize that they have common goals and expectations. Cooperation founded on common goals and expectations is the basis for synergy among human beings; therefore, cooperation between these traditionally opposing forces is more likely to lead to meaningful actions than either group acting alone.

A value system that transcends the divergent problem between the ecosystem and the economic system must rise above the growth-versus-no-growth, means-versus-ends dichotomies that characterize it. Which values will guide strategic managers on a clearer path toward making successful economic decisions within the limits of the Earth? What can managers use to define the ecological goalposts that delineate the playing field for the game called making economically feasible strategic choices? The answer begins with sustainability.

Sustainability: The Transcendent Core Value

A cursory look at the solutions generated by applying linear thought processes to the divergent dilemma of balancing economic and ecosystem survival reveals very familiar political directions. "Economic growth forever and ever; environmentalism is a knee-jerk reaction to imagined problems" is a typical rallying cry of the political right. "Economic growth stinks; shut down the economy, especially if it's capitalistic" blares just as loudly from the left. Lester Milbrath makes it clear that neither left thinking nor right thinking will be particularly useful in transcending the economy/environment dilemma. In describing his own political ilk, Milbrath (1990) is fond of saying, "I'm neither left nor right; I'm out front."

To Milbrath (1989), being out front means replacing left and right thinking with ecological thinking based on the value of *sustainability*. He says that sustainable systems have five characteristics: (a) the ability to preserve a well-functioning ecosystem; (b) the ability to provide humans with goods and services necessary for a good life; (c) the ability to provide people with fulfilling work; (d) the ability to maintain economic justice; and (e) the ability to use resources at a sustainable rate. Sustainability is determined by the Earth's carrying capacity: the amount of economic activity it can withstand within the limits of the ecosystem. Therefore, sustainability is central to determining optimal levels and optimal types of economic activity; it allows people to determine levels of industrial activity, agriculture, and human development that can be maintained over the long run (Daly & Cobb, 1989).

As these characteristics suggest, sustainability focuses on a healthy economic system operating within a healthy social system operating, in turn, within a healthy ecosystem. Thus sustainability provides a framework for a value system that, when implemented in business organizations, will encourage environmentally sensitive and economically successful strategic decisions. Sustainability is a "core value," one which defines the essence or basic theme of a broad set of values. As such, sustainability needs to be supported by a set of "instrumental values," values that provide the means for implementing the core value (Milbrath, 1989). People tend to have only a few core values, but each core value is usually represented by several instrumental values. For example, democracy is a core value that may be supported by instrumental values of voting, staying informed, and communicating with public officials. Again quoting Milbrath (1989):

> Maintaining the integrity and good functioning of its ecosystem should be the most fundamental value in the value structure of a sustainable society. Without a viable ecosystem, life cannot be sustained, society cannot function, and it will be impossible to realize quality in living. (p. 35)

Because the Earth has a limited carrying capacity, sustainability is a matter of scale. Growth in the scale of economic activity puts more stress on the ecosystem. Thus incorporating a value for sustainability into strategic decisions encourages managers to ponder what scale of activities is best in terms of those activities' environmental impact (Daly & Cobb, 1989). The Earth's limits also suggest that sustainability is a matter of efficiency; therefore, valuing sustainability encourages managers to constantly explore more efficient ways to use energy and resources in the production and distribution of their goods and services.

Using sustainability as a decision-making criterion encourages strategic managers to look beyond the boundaries of the organization and into the greater community in which it operates. The implications of this for strategic decision making are enormous; it improves the organization's ability to reflect the moral dimensions of society in their decision-making processes (Daly & Cobb, 1989; Etzioni, 1988). Questions about energy, resource use, pollution, product quality, durability, and packaging can all be put into an ecological perspective, and the interconnections between the organization and the various stakeholders that support it (customers, shareholders, local communities, etc.) can be clarified and strengthened.

In essence, sustainability is an appropriate core value on which to base strategic decisions because it transcends the dichotomies of growth/no-growth and means/ends. Neither unlimited economic growth nor the elimination of economic growth benefits the planet or its human inhabitants, but sustainability allows economic activity that accounts for the Earth's limits. It allows for an economic system that does not degrade the environment and may very well benefit it. Further, people cannot continue using resources at current rates, but they also cannot quit using resources altogether. However, if the sustainable use of resources is adopted as a value, then the limits of the ecosystem would be accounted for in many business decisions ranging from choosing energy sources, to determining distribution channels, to designing the work carried on by employees.

Indeed, sustainability is already rising in both business organizations and environmental groups as a unifying force that is turning the attention of these groups away from the left and the right and toward the future of the planet. Sustainability was the theme of a recent conference sponsored by *Business Week*. Attending were 200 business executives, government officials, and environmentalists. During his opening address, environmentalist Gus Speth (1990), president of the World Resources Institute, said:

> The solution [to our ecological problems] is environmentally sustainable growth and development. Businessmen [and women], environmentalists, and politicians, all of us are going to have to forgo finger pointing and join together to make this concept of sustainable development a global reality. And happily, some companies have already started doing so. They know that no business enterprise can be economically sound for long unless it's also ecologically sound. (p. 2)

He was echoed later in the day by a representative of industry, Jane Hutterly (1990), environmental action director of S. C. Johnson & Son. She said:

> Industry and government must form partnerships with the environmental community to help [with badly needed] massive public environmental education. This is an area where industry and government and the environmental community can work together to turn our very deep-green attitudes into equally deep-green actions. (p. 22)

Instrumental Values for Achieving Sustainability

Sustainability defines the essence of a value system that can solve the divergent dilemma faced by strategic managers when they try to balance economic and ecosystem survival. It is the principle on which the ecological playing field of business can be defined. Implementing sustainability as a core value for making strategic decisions, however, requires that managers adopt a set of instrumental values that support their quest for sustainable strategic choices. The authors believe that there are five instrumental values necessary for strategic managers who wish to make decisions based on sustainability—wholeness, posterity, smallness, quality, and community.

Wholeness

We discussed in Chapter 3 that achieving a sustainable balance in our ecosystem is possible if the planet is viewed as an interconnected whole, a living system that can survive only if a balance is maintained among its various subsystems. Also, we discussed in Chapter 6 that holistic thinking allows organizations to avoid the linear thought processes that so often exacerbate organizational problems. Thus wholeness helps people recognize that all of the Earth's living subsystems are parts of a supranational ecological system. Wholeness also helps people remember that survival depends on successfully interacting with other living subsystems on the planet, because the whole cannot survive if its parts are destroyed. Further, because the whole is defined by how its parts interact with one another, valuing wholeness helps people to better perceive and attend to the relationships with other elements of the environment.

Rene Dubos, who developed the first antibiotics, provides an excellent example of how holistic thinking can be beneficial. Whereas most physicians of his time believed that the ability to cure and/or eliminate diseases rested in isolating organisms and breaking them down into their smallest components, Dubos believed that no living organism could be understood except within the context of its relationships with the ecosystem. He revolutionized the medical profession with his theories, postulating that human disease is not usually caused simply by the presence of some particular organism; rather, he showed that the causes of disease are related to how humans interact with their total environment. Dubos believed that human health would not improve significantly until humankind learned to understand and sustain its environment. Because people have to adapt continuously to things such as increasing crowding and environmental pollution, he thought that serious disease of some type would always be present in society. Dubos's development of antibiotics resulted from his holistic perspective on the problem of controlling infectious diseases. He decided that the solution to effectively fighting these diseases was to find substances that would destroy whole bacteria rather than specific cells. This insight led to one of the most important medical advances of the 20th century (Moberg & Cohn, 1991).

In his 16th-century essays, philosopher Michel de Montaigne (1580/1958a) elegantly appealed to the need for decision makers to adopt wholeness as a value. He believed that people could comprehend the true impact of their decisions only if they accounted for the wholeness of the Earth and their role in it. On this point, he said:

> Whoever calls to his mind, as in a picture, the great image of our mother nature in all her majesty; whoever reads in her face her universal and constant variety; whoever sees himself in it . . . like

> a dot made by a very fine pencil; he alone estimates things according to their true proportions. (p. 63)

Montaigne also believed that decision makers needed to realize that when they made decisions, their actions would always have an influence (usually negative) on someone else and/or something else. Again quoting Montaigne (1580/1958b):

> No profit can be made except at another's expense. . . . As I was reflecting on this, the fancy came upon me that here nature is merely following her habitual policy. For natural scientists hold that the birth, nourishment, and growth of each thing means the change and decay of something else. (pp. 48-49)

Thus Montaigne captured two reasons as to why valuing wholeness is advantageous for strategic decision makers wishing to achieve a sustainable balance between economic success and environmental protection. First, a value for wholeness provides strategic managers with the broad perspective they need to remain competitive in today's living, global network of business activity. Thinking of the world as an interconnected whole provides a much clearer understanding of the cooperative, participative relationships that organizations need to develop with their employees, customers, suppliers, and other stakeholders. It can also give strategic managers a better viewpoint from which to observe and analyze today's complex, dynamic, international business environment. Further, as Rene Dubos adroitly demonstrated when he discovered antibiotics by looking at the whole bacteria, holistic thinking is of tremendous benefit to novel, creative efforts. New products, new services, and new methods can all spring from the value of wholeness. Thus valuing wholeness can contribute significantly to a firm's economic success in a very competitive world.

Second, Montaigne makes it clear that if people think holistically, they can't help but recognize and consider the impact of their decisions on other parts of the ecosystem. Understanding (a) where the organization fits into the ecosystem, and (b) that most organizational actions have some negative effect on other subsystems of the planet can give strategic managers an ecological perspective on which to base their decisions. They will be more likely to examine the impact of their decisions on other people, communities, societies, and the Earth. No doubt, wholeness is a value that, if adopted by strategic decision makers in organizations, would contribute significantly to sustaining the Earth's ecological balance.

Posterity

"We didn't inherit the Earth from our parents; we borrowed it from our children." This well-known Kenyan proverb clearly describes why posterity is an important value in order to achieve sustainability. Valuing posterity, believing that future generations of human beings are prominent factors in strategic decisions, can be instrumental in attaining a sustainable economic and ecological balance. Again quoting Gus Speth (1990), sustainability can be achieved only if society can attain "economic development that meets the needs of present generations without compromising the ability of future generations to meet their own needs" (p. 2).

People who grew up in middle-class America during the 1950s and 1960s remember the magnificent portrait of the American dream painted by their parents. "We want things to be better for you than they were for us," they said. This positive portrait, based primarily on economic wealth, provided the impetus for members of that generation to work very hard in order to achieve their economic goals. Unfortunately, the future does not look as bright for the current generation of children as it did for the previous one, and the environment is a major reason why. A Louis Harris survey concluded that 81% of the American public believes that the world will be a worse place to live 50 years from now because of the deteriorating environment. The youth are saying the same thing. In a recent poll by *Seventeen* magazine, 14- to 21-year-old Americans identified the environment as their number one concern, and a UCLA survey of its freshman class found that 86% of them did not believe that the government is doing enough about our environmental problems (Research Alert, 1991). An image of society based on unlimited economic growth has caused humankind to fall into ecological traps, raising serious concerns about the quality of life for our future generations. Assuming social scientists are correct in concluding that a positive image for future generations is critical to the survival and health of a society, there is every reason to be concerned.

Ornstein and Ehrlich (1990) make it clear that people's picture of the future will have to change drastically if they wish to develop a positive view for their children and their children's children. It may help if people realized how old (or young) humankind really is. The Earth is 4.5 billion years old, but human civilizations did not appear until 10,000 years ago, written histories began only around 5,000 years ago, and the industrial age has barely reached 300 years. Milbrath (1989) effectively demonstrates the significance of these time periods by envisioning a 1-year movie encompassing the Earth's entire history. If the movie began on January 1, dinosaurs would not appear until December 13, mammals would enter the scene on December 15, and Homo sapiens would make their movie debut at 11 minutes before midnight of December 31. Civilized human activity would not emerge until the last 2 minutes of the movie, recorded history would begin 1 minute before the curtain comes down, the industrial age would dominate only the last one and a half seconds, and our own lifetimes would flicker by during the final half second of the film. Maybe this movie can help put what is called long-range planning into its proper perspective.

Valuing posterity is an important ingredient in effectively managing the change and turbulence that all organizations now face and will continue to face in the 21st century. Adopting posterity as a value encourages business organizations to develop a vision of what they are and what they want to become. Having a clear vision of the future has proven to be a critical factor in successful organizations. Visions serve as common denominators around which strategic decisions are shaped and implemented. Shared visions in organizations encourage employees to think strategically; when strategic thinking is a part of an organizational culture, the company is better prepared to manage its opportunities and threats in ways that are advantageous to its survival and prosperity (Ernst & Baginski, 1989/1990).

The ability of the Japanese automobile manufacturers to capture a large percentage of the U.S. market exemplifies how valuing posterity results in high levels of customer loyalty and repeated business. It is well documented that one of the major advantages the Japanese have over U.S. automobile companies is their patience in waiting for investments to pay off. They invest large amounts of money knowing that they will not reap profits for many years. This is communicated effectively to customers; the preference for Japanese cars seems directly related to customers' perceptions that the manufacturers and the dealers have long-term commitments to innovative, high-quality, long-lasting products and services. Recently, Honda introduced four-wheel steering on its Prelude, though the firm knew that any profits from this development were at least 5 years away; in contrast, before he retired, General Motors CEO Roger Smith said that GM would not introduce four-wheel steering until it became profitable. When four-wheel steering becomes a viable option, which manufacturer will likely reap the most benefits, the company that has spent years developing, refining, and promoting it, or the Johnny-come-lately?

In addition to supporting economic sustainability, posterity is also important in order to achieve ecosystem sustainability. In strategic decision making, taking future generations into account significantly influences a wide range of choices. If strategic managers believe that clean water, clean air, abundant resources, and natural beauty are the birthright of all generations, not just their own, then the decisions they make are bound to better reflect a concern for the Earth. The Iroquois Indians had a seven-generation planning horizon; they tried to predict the effects of their decisions for the next seven generations to follow. This type of long-range planning by business organizations would tremendously enhance the sustainability of our small planet.

Smallness

As we discussed, sustainability is a matter of scale. Humans live on a small planet, one that is becoming overburdened with population increases and economic activity; thus thinking in terms of a smaller scale seems necessary. Thinking small will likely be difficult to accomplish. Daly and Cobb (1989) say that the conviction, bigger is better, is a deep social ideal that permeates the hearts and souls of most people today; changing the value of bigness will mean examining the basic differences between wants and needs in society. Of course, Schumacher (1973) brought the world's attention to the ideal of smallness. He said, "Small-scale operations, no matter how numerous, are always less harmful to the natural environment than large-scale ones, simply because their individual force is small in relation to the recuperative forces of nature" (p. 36).

Economic scale is ultimately defined by the amount of energy and resources transformed from their natural state into outputs, including wastes (Daly & Cobb, 1989). Thus valuing smallness has implications for every aspect of the economic cycle. At the production end of the cycle, smallness helps managers account more accurately for the value of the scarce natural resources that form the foundation of all economic capital. Smallness encourages strategic decision makers to implement policies aimed at using as little as possible of the Earth's nonrenewable resources. Organizations applying smallness to their strategic decisions are more likely to focus attention on searching for ways to save energy and to use more renewable energy sources in the production and distribution of their products and services. Smallness will also encourage organizations to look for ways to reduce the materials that go into their products, including packaging.

Valuing smallness in the production of goods and services has tremendous implications for the technologies used by organizations. Renewable energy technologies would obviously emanate from such a value. Also, organizations would require appropriate technologies designed to conserve resources, use recycled materials and energy, be less wasteful, and so on. Further, technologies would have to be developed to help deal with the massive wastes that are a part of the system for years to come regardless of action taken now. Because many advances in technology come from industry, technological development would provide many business opportunities for the 1990s as humankind strives to see "human technologies functioning in an integral relationship with Earth technologies" (Berry, 1988, p. 65). Among the participants of the *Business Week* conference on the natural environment, there was unanimous agreement that new environmental technologies will provide many business opportunities for decades to come (Brown, 1990; Sarney, 1990).

The value of smallness may have even greater implications for the consumption end of the economic cycle. As was gleaned from the industrial metabolism model (Chapter 3), the vast majority of the waste generated in society comes at this end. Developing more energy and resource efficient production and distribution processes alone will not lead to economic sustainability; these need to be coupled with efforts to consume less. Thus adopting smallness into the strategic decision-making process involves the consumer as well as the producer.

No doubt, as Daly and Cobb (1989) warn, moving from a culture based on bigness to a culture based on smallness will not be easy. However, as we have discussed, smallness is already emerging as a basic consideration in the way business is being done. Peters and Waterman (1982) repeatedly found that the efficiency provided by smallness was consistently profitable for the companies they investigated. Organizations are discovering the economic benefits of small work teams, energy efficiency, and smart growth; industries (such as waste management) that deal with the deleterious effects of bigness show promising opportunities for the future. Further, there is evidence that consumer values are also beginning to be redefined; green consumerism and ethical investing (which we will discuss thoroughly in the next chapter) are emerging as major trends influencing the business cycle. As smallness becomes a more significant influence on both the production and consumption sides of the economic formula, there is a distinct possibility that the resulting synergy may lead to smallness dominating our social consciousness in the same way that bigness does now. If this can happen, then both economic and ecological sustainability will be achievable.

Quality

Robert Pirsig (1974) engaged in a fascinating (and often frightening) search for the true meaning of quality in *Zen and the Art of Motorcycle Maintenance.* His schizophrenic inquiry led him to the conclusion that quality does not result from something people do or see; it is not an objective measure; rather, it is a perception with deep cognitive roots. This conclusion disturbed him; quality is, no doubt, a subjective mental image, but its basic purpose is to improve objective awareness of the world, that is, to provide observable criteria for making choices. How can it possibly be both subjective and objective? His final breakthrough (as well as his mental breakdown) came when he realized that quality could not exist either solely as a subjective mental picture or solely in the objects of the real world; quality existed in the interactions between the mind and its surrounding environment. He says:

> Quality couldn't be independently related with either the subject or the object but could be found only in the relationship of the two with each other. It is the point at which subject and object meet. Quality is not a thing. It is an event. (p. 239)

This perspective on quality is rapidly becoming the standard in industry. Quality today is becoming less and less the exclusive bailiwick of quality control engineers applying absolute standards and, instead, is more and more being determined through interactions between executives, operational employees, customers, suppliers, quality control personnel, and others. Quality, according to this definition, is not an absolute percentage of defective products, and so forth; rather, it is an overall perception of what the firm's products and services should be. As such, quality serves as the guiding force behind the firm's operations and its relationship with its stakeholders.

Primarily because of the influence of Edwards Deming, the Japanese initiated this trend toward an interactive definition of quality with their philosophy that quality is defined by the customer. This philosophy leads to the formation of strong customer-organization-supplier networks that are cemented by a shared vision of quality. Essentially, in relation to its products and services, an organization makes a concerted effort to identify customers' perceptions of what constitutes quality. These perceptions are passed on to operational employees who use them as guides for continuously improving the firm's products and services. Also, these perceptions are instilled in suppliers so that they can include them in producing the parts and services they provide to the organization. Thus the perception of quality in this process begins with the customer, but it transcends its roots and serves as an overriding image that determines the relationship between the organization and its stakeholders.

As an instrumental value supporting sustainability, quality is essentially the corollary of smallness. That is, changing from valuing bigness to valuing smallness dictates a value change from quantity to quality. Once organizations adopt the philosophy that how well products are made and how well customers are served is more important than how many products are produced and how many are sold to customers, then the proper scale of their operations can be defined by something other than physical growth: It can be defined by an overriding image of quality based on the perceptions of customers.

As organizations learn that they cannot be all things to all people, smallness will very likely result from a focus on quality. When quality is the nucleus around which organizations revolve, they are likely to adopt a scale of operations small enough to focus on developing individual relationships within their stakeholder network. Further, as the United States has learned (often painfully) from the Japanese, improved customer loyalty, more stable supplier relationships, more participative interactions among organizational members, and improved operational efficiency are all possible outcomes for organizations that adopt quality as a key value in their strategic decision-making processes.

The value, quality, best supports sustainability if it includes three basic dimensions—quality of products and services, quality of work, and quality of life. As we discussed above, the economic well-being of the firm is enhanced by improved customer loyalty, increased efficiency, and so on, that come with high-quality products and services. Quality products and services also support ecological sustainability because they last longer, are worth repairing, and can be exchanged more readily in second-hand markets such as flea markets and garage sales. A preponderance of durable, long-lasting products in the economic system will help to reduce the perception that constant style changes are necessary; high-quality products will also help to reduce wastes because fewer of these products will enter the system and more of them will remain in the system for longer periods of time (Daly & Cobb, 1989). Thus high-quality products and services are definitely important for achieving a sustainable balance of economic activity and ecological protection.

Attaining the sustainability promised by focusing on quality products and services is not possible unless organizations also value quality of work over quantity of work. Quality products and services are simply not possible without quality work. As discussed in Chapter 6, structuring jobs around the concept of good work, work that satisfies human needs as well as organizational needs, can improve the quality of products and services. This is because good work encourages employees to be creative and to contribute their best efforts to accomplishing the organization's economic goals and objectives. Further, the psychological satisfaction that people derive from good work often reduces their desire to consume more and more goods. As Daly and Cobb (1989) say, "Satisfaction derived from work is of equal importance with satisfaction derived from consumption" (p. 305). Thus good work also contributes to a sustainable economic-ecosystem balance.

Achieving sustainability via quality is also enhanced by valuing the quality of life in general; valuing the quality of life encourages strategic managers to recognize that all of their stakeholders have rights to physical well-being, long-lasting happiness, personal fulfillment, and a hopeful future (Milbrath, 1989). Such a value focuses the attention of strategic decision makers on how intricately interwoven economic sustainability and ecosystem sustainability really are. Valuing quality of life brings a wide variety of economic and environmental issues to the attention of organizations, including job design, organizational reward systems, employee health and safety, shareholder wealth, community economic development, pollution, waste control, and so on. This range of issues provides managers with the overall perspective they need to balance their economic activities with the limits of our small planet.

Community

Communities are not simply groups of people occupying patches of land. They are complex social systems composed of diverse individuals and organizations. Communities share at least three characteristics: (a) the members are conscious of their relationships with others in the community; (b) the members are conscious of the limits of the community; and (c) the members are conscious of the differences between themselves and those who live outside the community (Daly & Cobb, 1989). Thus, although communities usually share a common geography, the essence of a community lies primarily in the complex cognitive networks that form around the values and expectations of the individuals and organizations that comprise it. As Etzioni (1991) says, communities are identified by their "sense of we-ness" (p. 5).

Because communities are more cognitive than physical, they exist in many forms. Terms like local community, business community, religious community, and European Community all fit into the definition of community. In this sense, there is no need to differentiate between the terms community and society; communities simply represent the underlying social form on which societies are based (Daly & Cobb, 1989). Etzioni (1991) says, "Communities exist like Chinese nesting boxes, in that smaller ones—families—are embedded in more encompassing ones—say, villages—and these in still more encompassing ones—some national societies" (p. 5).

The shared values and expectations that make up the essence of communities lead to their strongest influence, establishing ethical standards. As physicist Werner Heisenberg once said, "Ethics is the basis for the communal life of men" (1985b, p. 44). Communities themselves have no power to coerce people to behave in socially acceptable ways (communities may have police forces with coercive powers, but the powers of the police result from shared community values for law and order, public safety, etc.); however, the moral codes of communities serve as public barometers by which the behaviors of individual members are judged and controlled (Etzioni, 1991).

As we discussed when we explored the field of economics in Chapter 5, many ecological problems stem from the neoclassical doctrine of radical individualism, the belief that serving one's self-interests necessarily results in the collective good. Throughout the book, we have fostered the opposite notion: Individuals, organizations, and economies are parts of a greater community; thinking only of themselves leads to individual actions that are detrimental to the encompassing systems of which they are a part. Daly and Cobb (1989) say, "In the real world the self-contained individual does not exist" (p. 161). They reject the idea that organizations are like Robinson Crusoe, earning their way solely on their own guile, in favor of the belief that organizations are integral parts of interlocking communal systems composed of individuals, families, towns, cities, nations, international coalitions, and ecological systems bound by a common desire for a high quality of life.

Thus strategic managers who value the greater community are better equipped to make decisions compatible with achieving sustainability. Strategic managers who adopt a value for community will better understand that the survival of their organization depends on their ability to serve the needs and follow the ethical standards of the more comprehensive communities to which they belong. Strategic managers who value community will also be aware that the community's survival depends on business organizations that contribute to a viable economy. Thus they are more conscious of the interconnections between their decisions and the quality of life in the communities in which they operate. They recognize that their organizations can prosper over the long run only if the community can maintain a balance between a healthy natural environment, ample opportunities for human development and fulfillment, a meaningful code of ethics, and a healthy system of economic activity. Accordingly, strategic managers who value community will likely benefit from numerous economic advantages such as customer loyalty, positive public image, and employee commitment as well as contributing to the protection of the natural environment.

Conclusions

Following strategic managers through their economic success versus ecosystem viability dilemma leads to the realization that the answers lie neither to the left nor to the right on the political spectrum. The answers lie in front, in finding the middle way—the path to a sustainable balance between the seemingly polar opposites of economic and ecological survival.

Solving the dilemma begins with instilling a set of values in business organizations that transcend this divergent problem, values that will help strategic managers recognize that the natural environment and success in business are not mortal enemies. Sustainability forms the core of this value system because it provides a foundation for making economic decisions compatible with the carrying capacity of the planet. Because they help to focus managers' attention on alternative solutions that transcend their dilemma, instrumental values such as wholeness, posterity, smallness, quality, and community can serve as the pathways through which sustainability is achieved

As we proceed from this point, two important questions remain. First, are there market forces currently emerging that will make it beneficial for business organizations to incorporate these values into their strategic decisions? Second, if such market forces are indeed present, what types of strategies can organizations implement in order to take advantage of them? We will explore these questions in the final two chapters.

Chapter 8

The Green Stakeholders

Central to the new management paradigm is satisfying the needs of the firm's stakeholders. As we discussed in Chapter 6, the Earth is the ultimate stakeholder in business organizations because of the environmental problems it faces and because it is the only real source of economic capital. However, because the Earth responds to the actions of business organizations at slow, evolutionary speeds, this is not, by itself, reason enough to encourage most firms to adopt the values of sustainability. Pervasive adoption of these values is unlikely to occur unless business organizations perceive that it is in their short-term as well as their long-term interests to do so. It may not always be economically feasible for organizations to respond to the cries of the planet alone. However, when other, more immediate, visible stakeholders such as customers, investors, and the political/legal system add their voices, the prospects for both short-term and long-term organizational success can be tied directly to adopting the values for a small planet.

What Do We Mean by "Green"?

The word "green" has become so popular that society seems trapped in a St. Patrick's Day dream. Green parties, green consumers, and green products are spewing forth like green beer in Chicago every March 17. Green is even being used as a verb; not only can something be green, it can also be greened. But what does green really mean? What is a green consumer, a green product, a green investment, or a green strategy?

The term *green* has been employed for years by environmentalists; its obvious connection to the colors of the Earth symbolizes environmentalists' strong concern for sustaining the planet. Recently, however, greenness has expanded beyond these relatively narrow roots into the general population. Opinion polls indicate that between 75% and 96% of Americans consider themselves green (Hayes, 1990; Kleiner, 1991b). However, only a small percentage of Americans are active in environmental organizations; only 12% give money regularly to environmental groups, and only 8% attend meetings regularly (Research Alert, 1991). The vast majority are "main-street environmentalists," people with little or no involvement in environmental organizations who nonetheless are concerned that no harm come to the natural environment as a result of their activities (Bell, 1990, p. 19). A full 57% of Americans say that they have made changes in their daily lifestyles that reflect their concern for the Earth (Research Alert, 1991).

The term green is essentially synonymous with ecological sustainability. Something is considered green if it meets five basic criteria: (a) it does not harm the health of people or animals; (b) it does not harm the natural environment; (c) it does not consume a disproportionate amount of energy or resources; (d) it does not cause excessive amounts of unusable wastes; and (e) it does not harm endangered species (Elkington, Hailes, & Makower, 1990).

The act of greening is the process of building these five criteria into products, business strategies, life-styles, and so forth. However, as Montaigne admonished, people's actions usually have negative effects on something else, meaning that it is all but impossible to achieve perfection in all five of these criteria. Therefore, green is especially difficult to achieve; it involves a number of complex choices and trade-offs. Thus there are many shades of green. As Ginny Carroll (1991) states, "Greening comes in more shades than an Irish hillside, from sickly chartreuse to deepest emerald" (p. 24). Green is, thus, an ideal state, and greening is the continuous process of moving toward that ideal state.

The Greening of the Immediate Business Environment

The stakeholders in the immediate business environment of organizations can be thought of as a plethora of carrots and sticks motivating strategic decision makers either by enticing them with the sweet taste of economic gain or by threatening them with the sting of economic penalty. Consumers can certainly be carrots; organizations pursue them with zeal, doing whatever they can to find out what they think, what they like, and what they want. Consumers can also be sticks; consumer boycotts (e.g., against Nestle) are excellent examples of using consumer power to motivate organizations from the rear. Ditto for investors; their money speaks as loudly as consumer dollars, drawing organizations to them like bees to honey, but they can also use tools such as proxy power to force organizational actions. The most feared stick is carried by the political/legal system, but this system offers carrots as well. Worrell and Gray (1985) point out that regulations often offer advantages for organizations, such as limiting competition by increasing costs, and Porter (1991) contends that strict environmental laws are competitive advantages in the global market.

Consumers, investors, and the political/legal system are all going through a greening process. This trio of major business stakeholders is beginning to sing a common tune about expecting business organizations to protect the natural environment as well as earn their profits. Together, these stakeholders have a powerful influence on the greening of business strategy; they are the carrots and sticks that make incorporating the values for a small planet a profitable and desirable endeavor for business organizations.

Green Consumers

According to Faye Rice (1990) of *Fortune* magazine, consumers in the United States are becoming "demanding, inquisitive, [and] discriminating." She says:

> No longer content with planned obsolescence, no longer willing to tolerate products that break down, they are insisting on high-quality goods that save time, energy, and calories; preserve the environment; and come from a manufacturer they think is socially responsible. (p. 38)

A basic element of this consumer revolution is green consumerism; many have predicted that addressing the concerns of green consumers will be one of the most important issues business organizations will face in the 1990s (Kirkpatrick, 1990).

Essentially, green consumers are people who buy green products, use them as long as possible, and recycle the wastes. Green products are those that are of high quality, durable, made with nontoxic materials, produced and delivered using energy efficient processes, packaged in small amounts of recyclable material, not tested on animals, and/or not derived from threatened species (Elkington, Hailes, & Makower, 1990). Green products fall into a category referred to by consumer behavior scholars as "high-involvement" products. Products of this type serve as personal statements about the values of the consumers who purchase them; they are tied directly to the consumers' self-esteem (Etzioni, 1988). As such, green products are not bought simply for their utility; they are purchased because they send a message from the consumers to the manufacturers about the products.

Green consumerism is becoming a profound force in the marketplace. The numbers of green consumers are swelling by leaps and bounds. A survey done for the Michael Peters Group in 1989 found that 89% of Americans are concerned about the impact that the products they buy have on the environment; three-fourths said that they are more likely to buy products in recyclable or degradable packages, and 78% said that they will pay extra for such packaging; 53% of those surveyed declined to buy at least one product over the past year because of their environmental concerns (Research Alert, 1991; Schorsch, 1990). The majority of American consumers even believe that it is worth accepting a lower standard of living if it means protecting the environment (Research Alert, 1991).

As mentioned above, being green is no easy task; it is filled with complicated choices that have to be made with data that are often confusing and incomplete. Almost half of the consumers who are interested in buying green products believe that the environmental claims of business organizations are little more than marketing gimmicks (Schwartz, Springen, & Hager, 1990). According to Denis Hayes (1990), the father of Earth Day and CEO of Green Seal, Inc.:

> People want to buy the right things, but they don't trust most of the information that they get. . . . If you walk into a supermarket today, you tend to think that, "My God, we've reached environmental nirvana." Everything seems to be Earth-friendly, environment-friendly, ozone-friendly, degradable, biodegradable, photodegradable, natural, organic, recycled, recyclable—and it doesn't mean anything. People know it doesn't mean anything. (p. 18)

This sense of confusion has led to calls for organized, independent efforts to consolidate information and help simplify the choices for green consumers. Again quoting Denis Hayes (1990):

> What they [green consumers] are looking for is some kind of independent certification effort that they trust; something that has no conflict of interest; has no stock in the sales of any product; that comes in as an objective third party . . . and says, "This is good enough. This is environmentally acceptable." (p. 18)

These concerns have spurred the development of several programs in which independent organizations test the environmental safety of products and apply their seals of approval (sometimes called eco-labels) to those products that pass these tests. The Blue Angel program in Germany was the first ecolabeling program, beginning in 1978; Blue Angel symbols now appear on about 3,500 products, attesting to the product's recyclability, safe packaging, absence of toxins, and so on (Dadd & Carothers, 1990; Schorsch, 1990; Weber, 1990). Because it is not realistic to expect products to be perfectly green, Blue Angel seals are awarded by comparing products in over 50 categories; seals are given to the most environment-friendly products within each category. Canada instituted its Environmental Choice program, modeled after Germany's Blue Angel program, in 1989; Japan's Eco-Mark program, that provides labels for advertising as well as products, began in 1990; the Netherlands, Norway, Sweden, and France are all currently developing their own eco-labeling programs. However, the most far-reaching program now under consideration involves the entire European Community (EC), a market of some 330 million consumers (not counting the Eastern European countries that will likely join eventually). The EC is considering the establishment of a Pan-European Environmental Quality Label: The label would certify products that use fewer resources, emit less harmful emissions when they are produced, have longer product lives, and can be reused or recycled (Schorsch, 1990).

The labeling effort getting the most attention in the United States is Denis Hayes's Green Seal, Inc., a nonprofit organization that began issuing labels in the fall of 1990 (Weber, 1990). Like its European brethren, Green Seal is establishing product categories and attempting to identify the most environmentally sound products within each category; it uses a council of independent scientists to determine criteria by which categories are determined and products are measured. The eligibility of a product for a Green Seal is determined via life-cycle analysis, allowing scientists to test a product from cradle to grave; this helps to ensure that a Green Seal is awarded only after the total environmental impact of a product has been determined (Green Seal, Inc., 1990). Green Cross is another independent, nonprofit group that certifies environmentally safe products in the United States. The standards used to award Green Cross eco-labels are more stringent than those of Green Seal (some say unrealistically so). Many believe that competition between Green Seal and Green Cross could be detrimental to labeling efforts in the United States (Weber, 1990).

Eco-labels are still at an early stage of development in the United States; however, several publications exist that attempt to guide consumers through their maze of green choices. *The Green Consumer,* first published in 1988, is a very comprehensive and informative book about what products to buy and what products not to buy (Elkington, Hailes, & Makower, 1990). *Shopping for a Better World* was published in 1990 by the Council on Economic Priorities to provide a guide to green consuming in supermarkets (Corson, Marlin, Schorsch, Swaminathan, & Will, 1990). Also, Seventh Generation (a catalog-sales company that specializes in environmentally safe products) publishes the *Green Consumer Letter* once a month. These are but a few of many publications currently available to help people make well-informed choices as green consumers.

Organizations are already rushing to capture the hearts and dollars of green consumers. Green products were introduced between 1985 and 1990 at a rate 20 times higher than overall new product introductions (Schorsch, 1990), and in 1989 the number of products packaged in environmentally sound ways grew 30 times faster than all new packaged goods in the United States (Research Alert, 1991). Over one-quarter of the new household products introduced in 1990 claimed to be some shade of green (ozone-friendly, biodegradable, etc.) (Frierman, 1991).

Of course, most consumers buy their goods in retail markets; thus retail is the area in which focusing on green consumers will have the greatest environmental benefits. As Stuart Rock (1989), business editor of *Director* magazine, says, "The cutting edge of green consumerism lies in retailing" (p. 40). Green retailers (some new and others old but willing to change) are becoming numerous. For example, both Safeway and Kroger have made efforts to green their operations by selling reusable cotton shopping bags, stocking organic vegetables, providing recycling bins at their store sites, and so on (Rock, 1989).

Two of the most successful green retail firms are The Body Shop, a chain of cosmetics shops (supplemented with catalog sales), and Seventh Generation, a catalog-sales firm that offers a variety of products, including recycled paper products, energy efficient light bulbs, water-saving devices, and environment-friendly cleaning items. The Body Shop sells only biodegradable, environment-friendly cosmetics in recyclable packaging, never tests its products on animals, and pays its employees to donate half a day a week to some social cause. Since its beginning in 1976, The Body Shop's annual sales have grown between 40 and 50 percent per year and currently exceed $500 million; the firm now has over 500 shops in 37 countries (Greengard, 1990). Seventh Generation, which began operations in 1988, currently has sales approaching $10 million annually, but founder Jeffrey Hollender is as proud of the firm's environmental success as he is of its economic success. In 1990 alone, Seventh Generation customers saved about 249 million gallons of water, 15,000 trees, and avoided putting 41 million pounds of pollutants into the air by purchasing the firm's products (Seventh Generation, Inc., 1991).

Probably the most visible retailers to don the color green are Wal-Mart and McDonald's. Wal-Mart is putting labels on products that it considers to be more environmentally safe because of better packaging, and so forth (Blumenthal, 1989). It is also working directly with its manufacturers to modify their production processes, packaging, and product disposal in ways that will make the products more environmentally friendly. Wal-Mart is also soliciting suggestions from its employees and customers about how to improve its greenness (Fisher & Graham, 1989).

McDonald's, in an unprecedented alliance with the Environmental Defense Fund, has vowed to significantly reduce the 2.6 million pounds of wastes per day that it generates (an average of 238 pounds per day at each of its 11,000 restaurants worldwide). It began a polystyrene recycling program in 1989, but has since announced that it will phase out polystyrene containers altogether. It is also beginning to compost egg shells, coffee grounds, and food scraps, is planning to recycle all of its corrugated boxes, and is testing reusable salad lids, coffee mugs, and shipping pallets. McDonald's is not only becoming a greener retailer, but also has made a major commitment to becoming a green consumer as well. It has notified its corrugated box suppliers that it wants the boxes to include at least

35% recycled material by December, 1991 (Allen, 1991). In April, 1990, McDonald's initiated a program called McRecycle USA, in which it committed $100 million per year to purchasing recycled materials to be used for new construction, remodeling, and furnishing its restaurants; this represents 25% of McDonald's total annual expenditures in these areas. Environmental affairs Vice President Michael Roberts said, "We felt we could be a part of the end-user group to buy recycled products" (Eisenhart, 1990, p. 25).

In addition to the retailers themselves, many retail goods manufacturers are greening their products. Procter and Gamble, which by itself generates one percent of the solid wastes in the United States, is making a concerted effort to reduce the amount of wastes in its retail products; for example, it is putting Spic and Span in bottles made from recycled plastics, and it is offering many of its cleaning products in concentrated packets that can be mixed with water in refillable bottles (Bremner, 1989). Tuna manufacturers are another case in point. Sales of tuna were declining steadily because consumers were becoming increasingly concerned about dolphins being trapped in tuna nets. Because of this, Starkist decided to introduce dolphin-friendly tuna that was caught using fishing methods that do not trap dolphin. Almost immediately after Starkist announced its decision, Chicken-of-the-Sea and Bumble Bee followed suit (although Bumble Bee has been criticized for making some false claims in this regard), creating a significant green dimension in the tuna market in a matter of a few weeks. Other examples of manufacturer greening include both Coca-Cola and Pepsi (which are beginning efforts to recycle plastic bottles—Coca-Cola is also reducing the weight of its plastic bottles), Estée Lauder (which encourages consumers to return the containers from its Natural Origins line of cosmetics), and Faber-Castell (which does not use any rain forest woods in the pencils it manufactures).

As good as the news of green consumerism is for the planet, a couple of words of caution are necessary here. First, identifying green products is no easy task. Life-cycle analysis, the basic tool for determining a product's greenness, is far from being infallible. Accurately measuring and comparing all the environmental risks in a product's entire life span is fraught with uncertainty (Stipp, 1991a). This means, of course, that eco-labeling, for all its good intentions, does not guarantee that products will be environmentally safe (Dadd & Carothers, 1990). Second, not all of the so-called green products on the market are all that green; consumers need some way to separate truly green products from mere green marketing schemes. As we mentioned above, Bumble Bee tuna has been criticized because its dolphin-friendly tuna wasn't that friendly; Mobil Oil has been chided for claiming its Hefty trash bags were biodegradable; and American Enviro Products, which makes Bunny disposable diapers, has received a great deal of criticism for calling the diapers degradable when, in fact, only the plastic back sheet of each diaper and the packaging are degradable (Slaba, 1990). Greenness can't be simply another marketing gimmick; it requires a true commitment based on values for a small planet.

The importance of green consumerism in achieving a sustainable balance between the ecosystem and the economic system cannot be overstated. As was demonstrated in the industrial metabolism model presented in Chapter 3, the consumption end of the economic process is where most of the energy is lost and most of the wastes occur. Thus green consumers and the firms that genuinely cater to them are critical pieces in the sustainability puzzle.

Ethical Investors

As Amy Domini and Peter Kinder (1986) say, "Every investment . . . has an ethical dimension" (p. xi). The idea of using investment power for social as well as financial returns dates back to the 1920s, when various religious groups demanded that their money not be invested in "sin stocks" (liquor, tobacco, and gambling). In 1928 the Pioneer Fund of Boston began eliminating from its portfolio companies that had operations in any of these three areas. Since then, many funds have emerged that screen their portfolios along numerous ethical, social, and environmental lines. Religious organizations have continued to be major influences in the ethical investing movement; for example, the Christian Scientists began the Foursquare Fund in 1962, and in 1968 the United Methodist Church withdrew its $10 million portfolio from First National City Bank (now Citibank) because of its investments in South Africa. Today, the Interfaith Center on Corporate Responsibility invests funds totaling $25 billion from the pension funds of 220 Roman Catholic orders and 22 Protestant denominations (Council on Economic Priorities, 1991).

The social turmoil experienced in the United States in the 1960s was the catalyst for the rapid growth in ethical investing. Social activist Saul Alinsky garnered support from hundreds of Eastman Kodak shareholders (the group controlled almost 40,000 shares of voting stock) in 1966, demanding that the firm hire 600 additional minority employees; civil rights leaders lobbied Chase Manhattan and Citibank in order to stop their investing in South Africa; stockholders of both Honeywell and Dow Chemical used annual meetings as public forums to air their objections to the antipersonnel weapons and napalm these firms were producing for use in the Vietnam War. In 1968, a Jewish synagogue requested that Alice Tepper Marlin, a securities analyst in Boston, develop a "peace portfolio" for it. When she had developed the portfolio, Ms. Marlin convinced her firm to run a newspaper advertisement offering the fund to other investors; some 600 investors responded to the ad. This interest in the peace portfolio eventually led to the formation of the Council on Economic Priorities (CEP) in 1969, which provides social performance ratings for individual companies (Council on Economic Priorities, 1991).

As the term suggests, ethical investing is a broad concept that goes beyond environmental performance. In addition to environmental responsibility, the CEP evaluates corporations on criteria such as charitable contributions, advancement of women and minorities, animal testing, community outreach, and family benefits (Council on Economic Priorities, 1991). Further, ethical investing has an economic dimension; like any investment, ethical investments are designed to earn reasonable financial returns for the investors (Domini & Kinder, 1986).

However, recent polls show that protecting the environment is the most prominent concern of ethical investors (Lublin, 1991).

There are two basic approaches to ethical investing. The first involves investing in firms (or investing in mutual funds with portfolios of firms) that demonstrate a sincere effort to be socially and environmentally responsible. (Implicit in this approach is that firms with poor social or environmental records should be avoided or withdrawn from investment portfolios.) There has been a tremendous increase in the amount of money invested in this way; what was a $40 billion market in 1984 is now estimated at close to $500 billion. A small fringe market with low volume has emerged as a major opportunity for investment professionals. For example, the Calvert Social Investment Fund has assets of about $250 million, the Dreyfus Third Century Fund has $190 million in assets, and Working Assets boasts a fund of $215 million. Further, a number of mutual funds are beginning to appear that invest their money specifically in firms that are environmentally concerned or whose primary business is environmental clean-up and protection. Examples of these environmental funds include Merrill Lynch's Eco-Logical Trust, the New Alternatives Fund, and the Shield Progressive Environmental Fund (R. A. Rose, 1990). With the environmental services market expanding at 15 to 20 percent per year, funds such as these are predicted to experience major growth in the 1990s (Rauber, 1990).

The beauty of ethical investments is that they are good not only for the investor's conscience, but also for the investor's wallet. Returns on ethical investment mutual funds have consistently done as well as or better than the market in general. When the Dow Jones Average crashed 22% in October, 1987, the five top ethical investment funds lost only about 12%. In 1988, Lipper Analytical Services ranked 1,470 mutual funds, and 2 of the 10 best performers were ethical investment funds (Council on Economic Priorities, 1991). Between 1987 and 1990, the Calvert Managed Growth Fund grew at an annual rate of 17%, the Dreyfus Third Century Fund grew at annual rate of 27%, and the Working Assets Fund grew at an annual rate of 20% (R. A. Rose, 1990). The relationship between protecting the environment and enjoying economic success can certainly be established via ethical investing.

The second form of ethical investing involves the use of proxy rights and annual shareholder meetings to initiate changes in the social and environmental practices of corporations. The shareholder actions at Eastman Kodak, Honeywell, and Dow Chemical mentioned above began a flood of such activities on behalf of the environment and other social causes. Two shareholder resolutions were presented at the 1970 General Motors annual meeting that resulted in the company appointing the first African-American to GM's board, Lewis Sullivan (author of the famed Sullivan principles, guidelines for companies doing business in South Africa). From that point, the number of ethical proxy proposals at GM shareholder meetings increased exponentially; there were 111 such proposals presented at the 1983 meeting (Council on Economic Priorities, 1991).

Interestingly, the flood of proxy resolutions that were beginning to inundate organizations in the early 1980s led the Securities and Exchange Commission to issue a new set of regulations in 1983 making it more difficult for shareholders to introduce such proposals at annual meetings. These regulations set the minimum amount of voting stock that must be owned by those introducing proposals at either 1% of total voting shares or $1,000 in stock value, and they prohibit shareholders from introducing proposals during the first year they own voting stock. The regulations also require that proposals achieve certain levels of support in order to be reintroduced at subsequent shareholder meetings: For a second introduction, a proposal must win 5% of the vote, for a third, 8% (Domini & Kinder, 1986).

Universities have taken the lead in using proxy proposals to achieve social and environmental change. Harvard was vehemently criticized in 1972 for investing in the Gulf Oil Corporation, a company heavily involved at the time with the repressive colonial government of Angola. The investigation of these investments by Harvard eventually led to the formation of the Investor Responsibility Resource Center, a consortium of universities (Boston University, Cornell, Princeton, Stanford, Smith,

Dartmouth, and Oberlin, among others) and foundations (Carnegie, Ford, and Rockefeller). This group studies the ethical proxy proposals of corporations and reports its findings to institutional investors, environmentalists, and other interested parties (Council on Economic Priorities, 1991).

Ironically, probably the greatest impetus for the growth and maturity of the proxy proposal movement is also one of the most serious industrial environmental disasters of all time—the Exxon Valdez oil spill. As Ginny Carroll (1991) states, "[Exxon's] mishandling of the Alaska spill became a corporate wake-up call to upgrade environmental risk assessment" (p. 24). To environmentalists, Exxon seemed to be both naive and callous when dealing with the spill. Chief Executive Officer Lawrence Rawl did not go to the site immediately; the company had apparently ignored Captain Joseph Hazelwood's previous alcohol problems; and the company's disaster-control and clean-up procedures seemed slow, careless, and more concerned about monetary costs than environmental costs (Council on Economic Priorities, 1991). Exxon's lax attitude and efforts resulted in the formation of the Coalition of Environmentally Responsible Economies (CERES), a consortium of 17 environmental groups (including the Sierra Club, Friends of the Earth, the National Wildlife Federation, the National Audubon Society, and the Wilderness Society) and 16 social investment funds (including the Calvert Fund, Parnassus Fund, Working Assets Fund, and Franklin Research and Development Corporation). The purpose of CERES is to "set forth broad standards for evaluating activities by corporations that directly or indirectly impact the Earth's biosphere" (CERES Coalition, 1990, p. 7).

CERES has chosen proxy proposals as its primary vehicle for accomplishing its purpose. It has developed what it calls the "Valdez Principles," a set of broad principles designed to provide an environmental responsibility signpost for investors to follow when choosing among investment opportunities. The 10 principles deal with biosphere protection, resource sustainability, risk reduction, product safety, damage compensation, disclosure of environmental mishaps, appointment of environmentalists to board of directors and management positions, and annual self-audits of environmental activities. CERES is asking companies to sign these principles in order to signify their long-term commitment to the process of achieving environmental sustainability. Proxy proposals to adopt the Valdez Principles have been presented to the shareholders of the Southern Companies, American Express, Atlantic Richfields, Kerr-McGee, Union Pacific, and even Exxon. Though none of these proposals have passed, they attained more support on the first proposal than CERES ever dreamed possible. They received between 8.5% and 17% of the proxy votes cast by the shareholders of these firms, which is much greater than earlier efforts to pass the Sullivan Principles, for example, and more than enough to have the proposals reintroduced at future meetings (CERES Coalition, 1990). As these principles appear on more and more proxy proposals, organizations will feel increased stakeholder pressures to be more environmentally responsible.

Like green consumerism, ethical investing is not a simple, clear-cut matter. As we have mentioned, there are many shades of green, and there is no way for a firm to be 100% environmentally safe. For example, should investors put money into DuPont because it has announced that it is phasing out CFCs and developing substitutes, or should they withhold investments from DuPont because it is still the world's largest CFC producer? Should they invest in Procter and Gamble because of its concentrated detergents that save packaging, or should they avoid investing in Procter and Gamble because its detergents contain phosphates that pollute the water and the disposable diapers it produces are clogging landfills? At the present time, there is no formal definition of "socially responsible" provided by either the Securities and Exchange Commission or the National Association of Securities Dealers (Rauber, 1990). Investors need to carefully investigate potential eco-investment opportunities in order to determine those that are truly related to environmental concern. Just as there are publications to help green consumers, there are guides available for ethical investors. The most complete ethical investing guide is *The Better World Investment Guide* published in 1991 by the Council on Economic Priorities.

Political and Legal Pressures

Government regulation has been aimed at environmental ills for many years. Theodore Roosevelt made conservation a popular political issue at the turn of this century. The courts have long held business organizations liable for employee health problems resulting from exposure to dangerous substances like asbestos and coal dust, and the Environmental Protection Agency has existed for over two decades in the United States.

However, the greening of government got its biggest boost in Germany, not in the United States. In 1983, 27 members of West Germany's Green Party were elected to seats in the National Assembly (the *Bundestag*). The German Green Party had become frustrated with politicians on both sides of the left-right spectrum; they felt that neither group was interested in environmental protection, but only in perpetuating their own narrow self-interests. The symbolic effect of electing of these Green Party members went well beyond their actual voting power in the *Bundestag*. Although the government wanted to seat them to the left of the liberal assembly members of the Social Democratic Party, the Green Party members refused. Instead, they insisted on being seated between the liberal Social Democrats and the conservative Christian Democrats. This gesture was important because it signaled a new political attitude for dealing with environmental issues. As Spretnak and Capra (1986) say:

> In calling for an ecological, nonviolent, nonexploitative society, the Greens transcend the linear span of left to right. . . . Greens have as their central concern and guiding principle the evolution of a new society based on ways of thinking and being that reflect the interconnected nature of all phenomena. (pp. 5-6)

Although no green political party has yet emerged as a force in U.S. politics (because of the inherent restrictions of the two-party system as well as political infighting and ineffectiveness among the greens themselves [Satin, 1990]), political officials and candidates from both the Republican and the Democratic parties are including the environment as a major part of their platforms. President Bush said he wanted to be the environmental

President, and to prove it, he appointed environmentalist William Reilly (former president of the World Wildlife Fund) to head the EPA, as well as pushing for passage of the Clean Air Act. United States Senator Albert Gore of Tennessee is probably the most staunch green political figure in the country today. Senator Gore has long been concerned about the environment; he served as a high school organizer for the first Earth Day in 1970 (Hayes, 1990). The environment has been the basic theme of his political rhetoric since his run for the Presidency in 1988; he recently visited polar regions with a group of scientists in order to witness firsthand the effects of global warming. He speaks of the need for broader taxes on carbon dioxide emissions and for increased government support of energy-saving technology. He says, "People aren't ready to believe that the challenge to the global environment is the most serious issue facing the world today. But it is" (Dowd, 1991, p. 120).

In the United States, the Environmental Protection Agency (EPA) has the primary responsibility for enacting, implementing, and enforcing federal environmental legislation. Created in 1970 as an independent agency of the Executive Branch, the EPA administers nine federal environmental laws. The more prominent of these include the Clean Air Act, Clean Water Act, Superfund, and Resource Conservation and Recovery Act (Environmental Protection Agency, PBS Adult Learning Satellite Service, and Public Television Outreach Alliance, 1990). The Occupational Safety and Health Administration is another federal agency with environmental responsibilities; specifically, it regulates the exposure of employees in organizations to toxic substances such as asbestos and benzene. The Federal Trade Commission (FTC) has also gotten into the environmental act; it has begun taking action against firms that engage in deceptive advertising practices concerning the environmental safety or friendliness of their products (Smith, 1990). This has led a coalition of trade associations representing more than 1,000 companies to ask the FTC for definitive standards about green labeling, and the FTC has responded by scheduling hearings on the matter (Frierman, 1991). Other governmental agencies involved in environmental protection include the National Forest

Service, the Bureau of Land Management, and the Fish and Wildlife Service.

Space does not permit us to discuss completely all of the environmental laws and regulations related to business activities. Managers need a working knowledge of laws, rules, and agencies that read like a bowl of alphabet soup—EPA, OSHA, RCRA, NIOSH, FTC, and so on. Further, many of the regulations are industry or situation specific and quite complex; how they affect specific firms depends on variables such as the production processes used, the types of products produced, packaging, shipping, and disposal. In other words, environmental laws regulate specific products in specific ways from their production to their disposal. Indeed, following these regulations can prove to be a nightmare for managers who don't pay close attention to them. One way for managers to keep up with regulations and to learn how to reduce pollution is to take advantage of the EPA's Pollution Prevention Information Clearinghouse (PPIC). The EPA also publishes a series of pollution prevention instruction manuals and has 11 libraries located in major cities throughout the country (Environmental Protection Agency et al., 1990).

Let's examine in some detail the 1990 Clean Air Act—the hallmark of the environmental efforts of the Bush administration. President Bush outlined six guiding principles for developing environmental programs that he says will maintain a healthy environment as well as providing for a healthy economy: (a) the power of the free market system should be used to achieve environmental protection; (b) pollution should be prevented before it starts; (c) a rich diversity of life should be maintained; (d) all environmental laws should be vigorously enforced; (e) environmental issues are global issues and thus require international efforts; and (f) joint public-private environmental initiatives should be encouraged (Deland, 1990). The 1990 Clean Air Act is designed to incorporate these six principles.

There are a total of 10 titles included in the new Clean Air Act. Title I establishes provisions for reducing lower-atmosphere ozone (smog), carbon monoxide, and particulate matter. Title II deals with mobile sources of air pollution; it mandates reductions of tailpipe emissions for automobiles and trucks (phased in over time), and it also mandates the development of cleaner burning gasolines. Title III directs that emissions of some 189 toxic air pollutants be reduced, Title IV seeks to reduce acid rain, and Title V enhances the monitoring and enforcement of standards by requiring organizations to purchase pollution permits. Title VI sets phase-out schedules for all chemicals that have been identified as dangerous to the upper ozone layer as well as those that have been shown to contribute to climate change (i.e., CFCs, halons, carbon tetrachloride, and methyl chloroform). Title VII specifies enforcement procedures and penalties for noncompliance with the act, Title VIII continues the federal acid rain research program, Title IX provides for additional unemployment benefits for those who lose their jobs because of the new regulations, and Title X mandates improved visibility near national parks (Environmental Protection Agency et al., 1990).

Title IV (the acid rain title) is probably the most innovative provision of the new law. Specifically, this title provides that sulphur dioxide emissions from power generating plants be reduced to 10 million tons below 1980 levels over the next decade. The novel feature of this title lies in its tradeable allowances provision. Each power plant is required to buy enough pollution allowances to cover its annual emissions. Plants that reduce emissions to levels below their allowed amounts can sell their excess pollution allowances to other plants whose emissions surpass their allowances, or they can report these excess allowances as assets on their financial statements. Thus Title IV provides positive market incentives in order for firms to commit significant financial and human resources to pollution control (Environmental Protection Agency et al., 1990). As we discussed in Chapter 5, economists such as Herman Daly have advocated approaches like this for years.

State governments are getting into the green act as well. Title V of the 1990 Clean Air Act encourages state governments to initiate their own pollution permit programs, and states such as Tennessee have already responded. California has the toughest air pollution standards in the nation, and it has decided to get even tougher. The California Air Resources Board has instituted automobile emission standards that get progressively tighter over the next 12 years. By 1996, many cars in the state will have to run on alternative fuels, and by 1998, 2% of the cars sold in the state will be required to emit no pollutants at all. This is quite significant because 11% of all the cars sold in the United States are sold in California. Further, New York, New Jersey, Massachusetts, and Maryland are likely to adopt some version of the California standards (Woodruff, Peterson, & Lowery, 1991).

Texas recently placed a temporary ban on the development of any new toxic waste sites or the expansion of any old ones, and Alabama, South Carolina, North Carolina, and New York are expected to follow suit. Governor Ann Richards of Texas said, "No more will hazardous-waste sites be rammed through the permit process over the objections of local communities" (Not in my backyard, 1991).

Packaging has also been a target of state regulation. Massachusetts is requiring that, by 1996, all packaging either be reusable at least five times, contain 50% recycled material, or be recycled at a 35% rate statewide; Maine has banned the sale of most drink boxes because they are not recyclable and thus detract from the state's recycling goals (Stipp, 1991b). These are but a few of the many efforts taking place at the state level to gain some modicum of control over environmental problems.

Private citizens are bringing environmental pressures to bear on organizations through the legal system. Those critical of environmental efforts still speak derisively of the notorious legal battles over protecting the tiny snail darter. Two very prominent organizations that have made major environmental strides by using legal channels are the Natural Resources Defense Council and the Sierra Club Legal Defense Fund. The protection of the northern spotted owl, which resides in the old-growth forests of the northwestern United States, offers a particularly well-known, current example. The Legal Defense Fund has brought forth a lawsuit to have the spotted owl declared an endangered species. Not only would such a move be good for the spotted owl, it would also protect many of the old-growth forests of the northwest from overharvesting by timber companies. So far the courts have sided with the spotted owl, but the battle continues. The Legal Defense Fund has also successfully brought the red-cockaded woodpecker into the fray (it ranges from Texas to Florida and up into the Carolinas), and there are plans to file for protection of the Mexican spotted owl of the southern Rocky Mountains (Turner, 1991).

The political and legal pressures on business organizations to protect the environment certainly do not stop at U.S. borders. Ecological problems are global in nature, and numerous nations and international organizations are making concerted efforts to regulate these problems. The vital influence of the green movement in Germany (exemplified by the success of the Green Party in the *Bundestag*) has led that nation to adopt some of the toughest environmental laws and policies in the world. We discussed Germany's development of the revolutionary "Gross Ecological Product" to replace the traditional GNP in Chapter 5. Also, a new German law (that goes into effect in January, 1993) will require a 30 cent deposit on all packages for drinks, cleaning products, and paints. Under the law, organizations will be required to accept used packaging from consumers, incineration of these materials will be banned, and recycling quotas will be imposed (Young, 1991).

German greens are also leaders of environmental reform in the entire European Community. According to Robert Hull (1990), adviser to the EC's chief environmental officer:

> There is now a very clear awareness in European-government circles of the need to protect the environment. . . . The environment has moved much closer to center stage of European Community policy thinking. . . . It is now inextricably bound up with economic strategy. (p. 8)

There have been approximately 150 pieces of legislation related to environmental protection passed by the EC, and strict enforcement procedures have been enacted to ensure compliance. Further, there are plans to institute a carbon tax for CO_2 emissions, to provide incentives for packaging reductions, and to create a European environmental agency to oversee the implementation of the community's environmental regulations (Hull, 1990).

The iron curtain tumbling down in 1989 was a dramatic moment in the environmental movement in Europe. Environmentalists in the iron curtain countries were at the center of the revolutions. As communist regimes fell in places such as East Germany and Czechoslovakia, the incredible ecological devastation they left behind became apparent. Dealing with the environmental problems in central and eastern Europe is one of the greatest challenges facing the European Community (French, 1990).

A number of other international efforts to protect the environment have taken place or will take place in the near future. The Montreal Protocol, signed in 1987 by dozens of industrialized nations (including the United States), set standards for protecting the ozone layer. In 1992, the United Nations Conference on the Environment and Development will be held with the express purpose of integrating ecological concerns into the economic policies of the UN (Benedick, 1990).

We could go on with this discussion, but by now the point should be clear. Political and legal pressures for environmental responsibility on the part of business organizations will not go away, nor will they slow down; instead, they will continue to get tougher. Most of the greening of the political and legal systems has occurred in the past 20 years, and the 1990s are being called the environmental decade for a reason. Strategic managers are faced with two choices: They can wait for changes in the political/legal environment and then react to them (the moving target of environmental regulation will make this a risky choice), or they can opt to become environmental leaders, anticipating political/legal changes and responding to them, when possible, before they are actually implemented. This proactive approach provides strategic managers with many economic opportunities in the future.

Conclusions

The growing presence of green stakeholders in the marketplace, who offer green carrots and wield green sticks, makes adopting the values for a small planet something other than a moral concern; it becomes a practical business concern as well. Organizational survival will increasingly depend on the firm's ability to meet the demands of these ecological components in the immediate business environment. So how do organizations respond to these segments of the market? How do they attract green consumers and ethical investment dollars? How do they profitably comply with increasing government regulations and avoid legal actions? They can begin by developing sustainability strategies designed to integrate environmental responsibility with economic success.

Chapter 9

Strategic Management for a Small Planet

Let's review for a moment. Humankind lives on a small planet, one limited in its ability to supply resources to and absorb the wastes of an exponentially growing population and an exponentially growing economic system. The planet is experiencing what are potentially catastrophic environmental problems. Air and water pollution, climate change, waste disposal problems, acid rain, and species loss are plaguing humankind; people's lives are becoming frantic and fractured; and these problems will likely get worse before they get better. Humankind can't stick its head in the sand and ignore what's happening; ostrich dynamics will solve none of these environmental problems.

Of course, there are many origins to these problems, and solving them will require efforts on many fronts. For example, education, population control, agricultural reform, technological change, and political change are all necessary. However, the most basic reforms are required in the economic paradigm. Further, economic reform means management reform because business managers collectively represent the largest group of economic decision makers. Indeed, our ecological problems are largely management problems.

In the 1990s and on into the 21st century, strategic managers will need new knowledge, new models, and new paradigms that allow them to guide their firms to economic success without putting undue stress on the ecosystem. It is necessary that they understand that the economic system in which they function is a subsystem of the living system called Earth. As such, the economic system is subject to the laws of thermodynamics, which define the Earth's limits for processing energy and wastes. Further, strategic managers need to understand that their values are critical factors in their decisions. Many of their current business values are based on unrealistic economic assumptions; they need to adopt new economic models that allow them to account for the Earth in their decision making.

A new management paradigm is beginning to appear. The new paradigm recognizes the true essence of the free enterprise system: No firm can prosper without serving the needs of its stakeholders; profits come to those firms that can successfully meet the demands of consumers, investors, employees, the political/legal system, and the greater social system in which they exist. Today these stakeholders are becoming decidedly greener in their attitudes toward business activity. They want less pollution and wastes, they want more recycling, they demand that more renewable energy sources be used, and they demand that products be safer for the ecosystem. Based on all of this, what should strategic managers do?

Strategic Management and Sustainability

Strategic management is a continuous process that involves the efforts of strategic managers to successfully fit an organization into its turbulent environment by developing competitive advantages. These competitive advantages should allow the firm to capitalize on its environmental opportunities and minimize its environmental threats. Thus strategic management involves continuously adapting to, and creating, change. The greening of the business environment is one of the most significant changes in recent times. Thus it follows that successful strategic managers in the decades to come need to adopt and implement strategies based on the core value of sustainability: strategies that address the interrelatedness of the ecosystem and the economic system.

The Vision of Sustainability

Strategic management begins with a vision of what the firm is and of what it will become. Based on the core values of the firm, this strategic vision is essentially an image that guides the firm's decision-making processes at all levels. The strategic management process involves developing the firm's mission, the goals and objectives it decides to pursue, the strategies it implements to accomplish its goals and objectives, the information it considers important, and the ways in which it measures its success around its strategic vision. Thus strategic management involves molding the firm's core values into actions that assure the firm's survival within its environment.

As we have discussed, sustainability means preserving the ecosystem as well as maintaining the ability to provide humans with the goods and services necessary for a good life, complete with fulfilling work and economic justice. Achieving sustainability requires determining which types of business activity fit into the Earth's carrying capacity and defining the optimal levels of those activities. William Ruckelshaus (1991), CEO of Browning-Ferris Industries and former head of the EPA, says that achieving sustainability in industrialized nations "means transportation without smog, consumer goods without toxic wastes, energy without acid rain" (p. 7).

Sustainability should be a core value because it supports a strategic vision of firms surviving over the long-term by integrating their need to earn an economic profit with their responsibility to protect the environment. Like a sailing craft in a race, the individual firm would see that the key to being competitive is the efficient and effective use of renewable resources. It would want to be as light and maneuverable as it could be, leaving no trace of its operations in its wake.

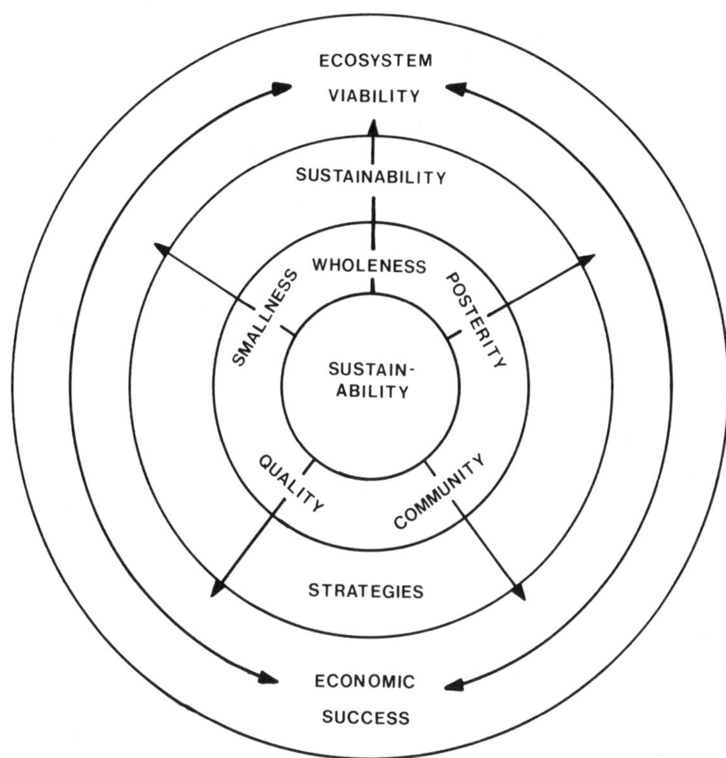

Figure 9.1. Envisioning Sustainability Strategies.

As can be seen in Figure 9.1, such a vision demonstrates the interconnectedness of economic success and the health of the ecosystem; the organization would see itself as a part of a greater society and natural environment, to whom its survival is tied. Thus this vision would serve as an excellent foundation for a strategic management process based on instrumental values such as quality, smallness, posterity, wholeness, and community. A firm with a vision based on sustainability would develop strategies designed to enhance its long-run profitability as well as to protect the ecosystem. We refer to these as "sustainability strategies."

Enterprise Strategy: A Framework for Sustainability

The concept of enterprise strategy has emerged in the past decade as a significant model for describing and analyzing the relationship between organizations and their larger environments. Igor Ansoff (1979) first used the term *enterprise strategy* while discussing the idea that, to be successful in the future, firms must achieve legitimacy within their social and political environments. Edward Freeman (1984) (who has probably contributed most to our understanding of enterprise strategy) says that enterprise strategy is a higher level of strategy that is concerned with what the firm stands for. He identifies three components for understanding a firm's enterprise strategy: (a) values analysis, (b) stakeholder analysis, and (c) issues analysis.

In 1988 Freeman and Gilbert explained that the concept of enterprise strategy ties business strategy to ethics. By determining what it stands for, a firm is able to explicate its purpose, and from that point the firm can develop a strategic management process that supports its purpose. They say:

> We propose the question "What do you stand for?" as one that must be answered alongside "What business are you in?" and one that will link ethics and strategy. "What do you stand for?" is an explicit appeal for a purpose, and as such, it forms a direct link between ethical reasoning and strategic reasoning. (p. 70)

Meznar, Chrisman, and Carroll (1990) point out that determining a firm's enterprise strategy requires an in-depth analysis of the breadth and scope of the firm's relationship with its various stakeholders; this means analyzing all of the benefits and costs (economic and social) associated with each stakeholder relationship. They say that a firm can increase its social value by decreasing its social costs and/or increasing its social benefits.

Enterprise strategy provides an excellent philosophical and practical framework for including the planet in the strategic management process. Philosophically, when a firm asks itself what it stands for and then consciously searches for the answer, it has an opportunity to gain a clear, in-depth understanding of the values that form the foundation of its ethical system. Significant clarification and modification of values will be necessary for most firms that wish to develop and implement sustainability strategies, and identifying the values on which the firm's strategies are based is the central focus of enterprise strategy.

Practically, enterprise strategy provides a very good analytical framework for developing sustainability strategies. If the Earth is included as a primary stakeholder in the firm, then Freeman's three components for determining enterprise strategy can be used to enhance strategic managers' abilities to develop strategies that recognize the relationship between the firm and the natural environment. First, values analysis assists strategic managers in assessing the degree to which sustainability has emerged as a core value of the firm and which instrumental value changes are required to fully adopt it. Second, stakeholder analysis helps strategic managers to better comprehend that the Earth is a stakeholder with tremendous breadth. The present human inhabitants on Earth would be incorporated as stakeholders in the firm, as would future generations of human beings and other species that exist on the planet; the systems that support life on Earth (the air, water, and land) would also be recognized as significant stakeholders in the firm's operations. Also, stakeholder analysis helps the firm to better understand the influences that green consumers, ethical investors, and the political/legal system have on the firm. Finally, issues analysis clarifies the relationship between the ecological issues facing the Earth and the strategic issues addressed by the organization. Strategic managers would be able to assess the impact of the firm's operations on the Earth's resources, species, and systems; the results of the assessment could then be incorporated into the firm's strategic decisions.

Thus, analyzing the values, stakeholders, and issues related to preserving the Earth permits strategic managers to more effectively incorporate these factors into the goals and objectives of the firm. Sustainability values would form the basis of the strategic management process, the costs and benefits of the firm's operations would be measured against the survival needs of the planet's stakeholders, and managers would choose sustainability strategies that allow the firm to operate in profitable, environmentally-sound ways.

Sustainability Strategies and Competitive Advantage

It is important to note that sustainability strategies are not compromise strategies; they are not designed merely to earn a profit while doing as little damage as possible to the ecosystem. Rather, they are integrative strategies; they provide competitive advantages to organizations by simultaneously enhancing the quality of the ecosystem and the long-term survivability of the firm. As Art Kleiner (1991b) says, "In the long run, the principles of economic growth and environmental quality reinforce each other" (p. 38). Michael Porter (1991) reiterates this point, saying, "The conflict between environmental protection and economic competitiveness is a false dichotomy" (p. 168).

In the front interface with its environment, in which a firm interacts with customers and investors, sustainability strategies can be used to gain an advantage over the competition in several ways. We saw in Chapter 8 that consumers and investors are increasingly demanding greenness on the part of organizations. We presented examples (Wal-Mart, Merrill Lynch's Eco-Logical Trust, etc.) of how organizations are thriving economically by appealing to these green stakeholders. Further, as Halal (1986) says, smart growth involves turning environmental threats into business opportunities. Many business opportunities exist in industries that are environmentally friendly or are involved in some form of environmental protection, and these opportunities will continue to increase over the next decade, providing fertile ground for a variety of entrepreneurial activities.

One example of smart growth is occurring in the recycling industry. As wastes and resource depletion have increased, the recycling industry has prospered; it is projected to grow between 25% and 30% annually between 1990 and 1995. Improved processes for recycling items such as plastics and disposable diapers are rapidly appearing on the scene (Nulty, 1990). Alternative energy sources are also providing smart growth opportunities. Luz International operates a 200 megawatt solar-thermal power generating facility in California that serves 270,000 people. National Energy Associates (NEA) provide power to between 15,000 and 20,000 people by generating energy from 260,000 tons (annually) of low quality cattle manure that cannot be used as fertilizer; the plant saves about 350,000 barrels of oil each year. The president of NEA, Will Parish, points out that this is no do-gooder venture; the firm has paid high returns in order to attract the $100 million in investments it has received.

In addition to recycling and energy, many other industries (such as organic foods and recreation) are providing smart growth opportunities related to our ecological problems (Growing greener, 1989). In 1991, *Ecopreneuring* by Steve Bennett was published; this book is a guide to green entrepreneurial opportunities in industries such as recycling, water treatment, travel, and entertainment. Also, for over a decade a magazine entitled *In Business* has been offering to its readers ideas about environmentally sensitive entrepreneurial opportunities.

At the rear interface with its environment, in which the firm acquires and uses the energy and resources to produce and deliver its goods and/or services, sustainability strategies can also provide several competitive advantages. Reducing the amount of energy and materials consumed in manufacturing and distributing a product or service not only reduces resource depletion, it also reduces costs. The same is true for reducing waste generation and effluent emissions. If production systems can be designed to resemble ecosystems, whereby their wastes and effluents serve as energy sources and raw materials for other processes, then pollution reduction and cost reduction can both be realized (Dougherty, 1990).

Another rear-interface focus that provides both ecological and economic benefits to a firm is the production of high-quality products. High "conformance quality" (quality based on carefully and precisely conforming to internal specifications) reduces costs because of lower scrap, less rework, less time spent responding to complaints, and so on. It also leads to superior "perceived quality" by customers, and, when customers believe that a product's quality is superior to the competition, a firm can experience higher customer loyalty, more repeat business, opportunities to charge higher prices, and market share improvements (Buzzell & Gale, 1987). Add to these economic benefits the ecological benefits that accrue from higher quality (such as the reduction of wastes in manufacturing processes and end-user disposal), and it becomes clear that focusing on quality is a natural strategy for firms concerned about their survival and the survival of our small planet.

In short, sustainability strategies can improve a firm's competitiveness for two reasons: (a) they result in lower costs, and (b) they give the firm the opportunity to differentiate itself and its products from its competitors. According to Michael Porter (1985), cost leadership and differentiation are the two basic competitive advantages firms can develop. Both of these are afforded by sustainability strategies, strategies that not only improve the firm's economic success, but also allow the firm to protect the Earth in the process.

Sustainability Via Total Quality Management

Sustainability strategies have begun to appear in a number of forms. In the last chapter, we discussed McDonald's front- and rear-interface recycling strategies designed to reduce costs and wastes and to improve its public image; we also discussed the safe-products strategies of Seventh Generation and the Body Shop. However, the most notable current trend in sustainability strategy development seems to be the move toward a total quality management (TQM) approach.

TQM and Environmental Management

Total Quality Management rests on the assumption that quality is defined by customers; TQM programs involve implementing organizational structures and processes that ensure that the firm consistently provides high-quality goods and services to its customers. There are six core principles that drive TQM programs: (a) effective relationships with customers and suppliers are central to defining and maintaining quality; (b) a firm's core work processes should be capable of consistently satisfying customers' perceptions of quality; (c) effective quality management requires increased use of measurable data and less reliance on instinct and experience; (d) effective quality management requires an organizational system that has a continuous focus on problem solving; (e) higher quality translates into higher financial returns for the firm; and (f) quality is everyone's job and can be achieved only through teamwork (Heilpern, 1990).

Understanding TQM means recognizing that it is more than a technique; TQM is a new way of thinking about quality. Peter Senge (1990) gives a very clear description of this:

> For years American manufacturers thought they had to choose between low cost and high quality. . . . What they didn't consider was all the ways that increasing quality and lowering costs could go hand in hand, over time. What they didn't consider was how basic improvements in work processes could eliminate rework, eliminate quality inspectors, reduce customer complaints, lower warranty costs, increase customer loyalty, and reduce advertising and sales promotion costs. They didn't realize that they could have both goals, if they were willing to wait for one while they focused on the other. (p. 65)

TQM provides a natural vehicle for developing and implementing sustainability strategies. Karen Bemowski, associate editor of *Quality Progress*, says that there are five misconceptions about the relationship between quality and the environment: (a) quality and the environment have nothing in common; (b) environmental problems are the bailiwick of environmental professionals, not line employees involved in producing the products; (c) measuring wastes means trouble for employees because the results can only hurt, not help, an employee's performance appraisal; (d) wastes that do not exceed EPA standards do not matter; and (e) tighter environmental regulations automatically translate into lower profits. She believes that applying TQM to managing the ecological issues of the firm will dispel all of these misconceptions. TQM integrates the two concepts by making total quality the ultimate goal of a firm's environmental management program. Implementing TQM requires that all employees be involved in the program, and it also requires that employees be positively rewarded when they contribute to improving the firm's environmental performance. Further, going beyond the minimal requirements of the EPA requires firms to reduce wastes and pollution, and reducing wastes and pollution has a positive impact on the profits of the firm (Bemowski, 1991).

The greatest impetus for the application of TQM to environmental management has been provided by the Global Environmental Management Initiative (GEMI). Having evolved from an environmental management group formed by the Business Roundtable in 1989, GEMI is an organization composed of environmental management practitioners whose basic aim is to promote environmental excellence within the global business community. It is currently working with the United Nations Environmental Programme, the International Chamber of Commerce, and the International Environmental Bureau to develop a global environmental management business ethic (Kelly, 1991).

The Global Environmental Management Initiative has a two-fold approach to accomplishing its mission. First, it attempts to heighten awareness that business organizations have a major role to play in cleaning up and protecting the environment. Second, it provides information and techniques to firms that are designed to help them improve their environmental performance by tying it to their economic performance (Kelly, 1991). TQM is central to GEMI's efforts. According to George Carpenter (1991), chief environmental officer of Procter and Gamble and chairman of GEMI:

> Environmental quality and total quality are complementary and synergistic concepts. . . . When businesses apply total quality to environmental management, they reap three basic benefits: an alignment with business strategy, continuous improvement with measurable results, and a customer and supplier alignment. (pp. 2-3)

GEMI held its first conference in January, 1991, attracting over 250 participants from many international companies.

Environmental officers from about 30 organizations (including IBM, Union Carbide, Square D, Merck, Browning-Ferris, Occidental Petroleum, AT&T, Digital Equipment, Procter and Gamble, and Dow) made presentations concerning the application of TQM to environmental management in their organizations. The approaches and techniques each firm used varied, but there were several general themes that ran through the presentations.

The first step that most of the GEMI participants described in applying TQM to environmental management was identifying the customers that the environmental units serve. All identified state and federal agencies such as the EPA and OSHA as customers of their environmental programs, and most identified employees and other units within their firms as customers of their services. Many went further and identified all the basic stakeholders that comprise the planet Earth. Says James MacKenzie (1991), director of corporate environmental health and safety for Xerox, "Xerox has become committed to the protection of the environment, conservation of materials and resources, and the health and safety of its employees, customers, and neighbors worldwide . . . " (p. 42).

There was consensus among the GEMI participants that tools and techniques that provide them with accurate, customer-focused information as to the progress they are making in their environmental management efforts are necessary. Environmental, health, and safety audits were suggested by most participants, and tools like fishbone diagrams, process flow charts, story boards, and statistical quality control measures were also mentioned a number of times as valuable in measuring the continuous environmental improvements they were seeking.

The GEMI participants were in agreement on a number of other points as well. First, TQM-based sustainability strategies require a strong commitment from top management in order to be implemented effectively. Second, the participative nature of TQM means that implementing TQM-based sustainability strategies requires significant education and training for all members of the organization. Third, firms have to be willing to invest the financial resources necessary to implement these strategies;

and fourth, firms need to develop structures that foster the participation and communication necessary to carry out these strategies. Because of the significant organizational culture and value changes involved, patience on the part of the organization is required. Interestingly, there is nothing unique about these requirements; they are necessary for effectively implementing any strategy.

Examples of TQM-Based Sustainability Strategies

Total quality management is becoming a standard process for implementing sustainability strategies in industry. Hundreds of major companies are currently practicing TQM in efforts to make good environmental performance a basis of good financial performance. Interestingly, the firm that was the pioneer in applying TQM to environmental management did so before the term was even popular.

In 1975, 3M (one of the world's largest polluters and waste generators at the time) began its Pollution Prevention Pays (3P) program. The program was designed to switch the focus of pollution prevention at 3M from the output end to the input end of the firm's production processes. Executives were convinced that preventing pollution before it occurred made a great deal of economic sense when compared with the high costs and inherent inefficiencies of scrubbing it, treating it, storing it, burning it, transporting it, and burying it after the pollution and wastes had been generated (Gold, 1990).

3M is currently saving almost $500 million per year because of the 3P program. These savings are coming from an annual reduction of 530,000 tons in air pollution, water pollution, sludge, and solid wastes, and a reduction of 1.6 billion gallons per year in waste-water generation. Further, the firm has implemented an energy conservation program that has saved it $650 million, and it is spending $150 million between 1990 and 1993 to install thermal oxidizers to further control air pollution. 3M's efforts have not gone unnoticed. It won the World Environment Center's first Gold Medal in 1985, and it was awarded the

Council on Economic Priorities' Corporate Conscience Award in 1988 (Gold, 1990).

AT&T is another prominent firm that is energetically implementing TQM-based sustainability strategies. In 1990, Bob Allen, chairman of the AT&T board of directors, announced that the firm intended to vigorously incorporate environmental concerns into all of its business activities. TQM was chosen as the primary vehicle for accomplishing this goal because it gets everyone in the company involved in satisfying its environmental stakeholders (Stratton, 1991). The environmental goals AT&T has set for itself are very ambitious. It plans to eliminate all CFCs from its processes by 1994 (the world goal is a 50% cut by 1998), and it plans to eliminate all air pollution by 2000. Also, it plans to achieve a 25% decrease in total manufacturing process wastes, a 35% increase in the amount of paper recycled, and a 15% decrease in the amount of paper used by 1994. AT&T hopes that these ambitious goals will set an example for other firms to follow. The firm wants to make it clear that this is more than a simple public relations trick. Says Art Soderberg, Chief Environmental Officer at AT&T, "It's not just for public relations; it's for the sake of the environment we live in and our children" (Stratton, 1991, p. 19).

Located in Greeneville, Tennessee, the Ball Zinc Products Division produces 70% of the nation's pennies. Early efforts in the firm's TQM-based waste reduction strategy led to a 38% reduction in the 18,000 pounds of toxic sludge generated daily at the plant. The installation of a new wastewater treatment system in July, 1990, permitted the firm to reduce its sludge generation an additional 52%. The firm currently generates 2,600 pounds per day, and recycles 800 pounds of this. Therefore, it only ships 10% of its original discharge (1,800 pounds per day) to off-site dumps. The cost to Ball Zinc was $750,000, and this investment has paid off handsomely; the Earth is being spared 16,200 pounds of toxins per day, and the firm is realizing an annual cost savings of $500,000.

Ball Zinc was awarded the 1990 Tennessee Governor's Award for Excellence in Hazardous Waste Management, along with

Great Dane Trailers of Memphis.[1] In 1987 Great Dane was annually emitting 224,000 pounds of toxic chemicals into the air and was shipping 123,000 pounds of toxic wastes from paint-related materials to off-site dumps each year. In February, 1990, the firm instituted process changes that have led to a 90% reduction in air emissions and a 100% reduction in paint-related wastes. The paint wastes are now completely recycled into a superior quality undercoat for the trailers, a product that was previously purchased from an outside supplier. As with other TQM-based sustainability strategies, the firm and the planet are both reaping the benefits; Great Dane is saving $135,400 annually.

The petrochemical industry generates billions of pounds of toxic wastes and pollution annually; this is a major reason why the industry has been under serious scrutiny for years. Images created by incidents like Love Canal, Bhopal, and Valdez have incessantly hounded the industry. Recently, a number of organizations in the industry have responded with TQM-based sustainability strategies. We mentioned that Union Carbide, Dow, and Occidental participated in the 1991 GEMI conference, sharing information with other firms about their programs; Ashland Oil, Vulcan Chemicals, and DuPont were also active in the conference.

Dow Chemical is a firm that has been maligned much over the years for its environmental performance (primarily because it produced both napalm and agent orange during the Vietnam War). However, it has emerged as a leader in its industry at applying TQM-based sustainability strategies. It has instituted a program called WRAP (Waste Reduction Always Pays). Examples of WRAP decisions at Dow include redesigning its catalytic converters, installing pipes that are more resistant to corrosion, and insuring that suppliers provide purer raw materials. The installation of the corrosion-resistant pipes has resulted in an annual savings of $890,000 to the firm as well as eliminating the discharge of hydrochloric-caustic cleansers previously used to remove corrosion from the old pipes. Dow cut its toxic emissions in half between 1984 and 1988, and in 1991 Dow ranked 29th among chemical companies in total emissions although they are the second largest firm in the industry (Kleiner, 1991a).

Among chemical manufacturers, Monsanto is another leader in its use of TQM to reduce pollution and wastes. It set a goal in 1988 to reduce its toxic air emissions by 90% by the end of 1992, and so far, it is on target. The company is also investing research dollars in a process called "bioremediation" (a process that employs natural substances to remove toxins from air, water, and land) that has the potential to be a more ecologically-sound and cost-effective technology (Stratton, 1991).

One of the primary reasons for the involvement of petrochemical companies in the development of TQM-based sustainability strategies is the stance taken by the Chemical Manufacturers' Association (CMA) in March, 1990. At that time, the 175 members of the CMA agreed to enact a set of guidelines designed to significantly improve the way firms in the industry managed the chemical manufacturing process. The CMA calls these guidelines Responsible Care. Eugene McBrayer, president of Exxon Chemicals and chairman of the CMA when the Responsible Care guidelines were passed, said, "The drive for continuous improvement toward a goal of completely error-free operations makes a lot of sense. And that's exactly what Responsible Care is intended to accomplish" (Stratton, 1991, p. 20).

There are nine Responsible Care guidelines: (a) to safely develop, produce, transport, use, and dispose of chemicals; (b) to make health, safety, and the environment priority considerations in planning for both current and new products; (c) to promptly report any chemical or health hazards and be prepared to deal with them if they occur; (d) to inform customers how to safely transport, store, and use chemicals; (e) to always operate plants in a safe manner; (f) to support research on the environmental impacts of products, processes, and wastes; (g) to contribute significant efforts to resolve problems caused by past practices; (h) to participate with the government to develop laws and regulations that promote a safer, more environmentally-sound industry; and (i) to share environmental management experiences and information with other firms in the industry (Stratton, 1991).

TQM-based sustainability strategies provide firms with the opportunity to find cost-leadership positions relative to the competition by reducing their resource, pollution, and waste-generation costs. They also provide firms with the opportunity to differentiate themselves from their competitors; these firms can offer their customers superior products and services, and they can appeal directly to green consumers and investors. No doubt, TQM-based sustainability strategies represent the leading edge of the current approaches to integrating economic and ecological goals in business organizations.

Barriers to Implementing Sustainability Strategies

It would be naive to believe that humankind is now on the brink of solving all the conflicts that exist between earning an economic profit and protecting the planet. What sustainability strategies (like those based on TQM) represent are the first tenuous steps on a long, rocky journey toward achieving true harmony between the economic system and the ecosystem. This journey is fraught with obstacles that are going to require tremendous effort and ingenuity to overcome.

Physical Barriers

As we discussed previously, the entropy law provides the absolute physical wall beyond which human activity on Earth is not possible; however, the activities humans decide to engage in while on Earth are critical determinants of how fast the entropic processes on the planet occur. In order to slow down the entropic processes that result from the current level of business activities, it is necessary to bridge several physical barriers. These include: finding safe and/or plentiful substitutes for nonrenewable resources and toxic chemicals now in use; developing the efficient use of clean, renewable energy sources; developing better processes for recovering, recycling, and disposing of wastes; and developing more efficient production processes.

One area in which technological progress is showing great promise in helping to overcome the physical barriers to sustainability is the development of renewable, nonpolluting energy.

The costs of renewable energy technologies have dropped between 65% and 90% (depending on the specific technology) since 1980; this trend is expected to continue into the next century as improvements are made in photovoltaic solar cells, hydrogen power, geothermal energy, and wind power. For example, Texas Instruments announced in April, 1991, that it plans to begin production of a smaller, more efficient photovoltaic solar energy cell that costs half as much to produce as current models. Many believe that photovoltaic cells will become small enough to be used as roofing material in the near future, decentralizing energy generation almost completely. Further, several large solar power plants will likely be built in deserts during the next decade that will require less space per kilowatt than current coal and nuclear plants. Hydrogen power is also showing promise. It is the most plentiful element in the universe, and in gas form it burns clean and can be transported with almost no energy loss (minimal entropy). Prototype hydrogen gas systems for cooking, heating homes, powering factories, and running automobiles already exist. California is leading the way in utilizing renewable energy; forty-two percent of the electricity generated in the state currently comes from hydrological, solar, biomass, wind, and geothermal sources (Flavin & Lenssen, 1991).

However, even with promising technological improvements such as these and the advent of approaches like TQM as means for reducing resource use and wastes in industry, many bumps still lie on the road ahead. For example, there are still no acceptable substitutes for CFCs. Although both of the world's largest CFC producers (DuPont and Imperial Chemical Industries [ICI]) have announced that they will phase out the chemical in or before the year 2000 (the date called for by the Montreal Protocol), the only substitutes they currently have available also deplete the stratospheric ozone (albeit to a lesser degree); DuPont and ICI plan to produce these substitutes for up to another 50 years (McCully, 1991). This is an ominous prospect because CFCs are very stable and will continue to do damage for 100 years into the future, even if production was stopped today (Graedel & Crutzen, 1989).

One of the more perplexing dilemmas faced by business organizations searching for ways to overcome the physical barriers to sustainability strategies lies in the conflicts that exist between certain social and environmental goals. One of the most notable conflicts exists between safety, quality, and energy/ resource conservation. This is an especially thorny issue in the automobile industry. We mentioned in Chapter 3 that dematerialization is a basic goal of automobile manufacturers; the less the car weighs, the fewer resources needed to produce it and power it. Unfortunately, less weight also presents the potential for safety hazards and quality problems (Herman, Ardekani, & Ausubel, 1989). This dilemma presents very difficult issues for strategic managers making decisions about automobile design.

The many complex physical barriers to implementing sustainability strategies indicate a strong need to continue research and development in environmentally sensitive production and energy generating technologies. This need for continued research means that organizations and governmental agencies need to be willing to invest the necessary time and money into such efforts. However, a more fundamental issue associated with this problem involves the fact that engineering schools at universities have traditionally done a poor job of incorporating environmental constraints into their curricula and research. A concerted effort is needed to better integrate the limits of the planet into the educational processes and research endeavors in all engineering disciplines if sustainability is to be achieved (Friedlander, 1989).

Social Barriers

As we have emphasized many times, environmental problems are global problems. Sustainability cannot be achieved if its strategies exist in only a few companies, industries, or nations. Achieving sustainability will require that economic enterprises all over the world adopt sustainability strategies. The complexities of such a task are enormous, bringing to bear some of the most crucial social issues related to the long-term survival of the planet. We discussed one of these issues in Chapter 5, the fact that many resource-rich, economically poor nations readily exchange their natural capital for financial capital although the practice devastates the environment and does little for the economic welfare of most of its citizens. It is critical that sustainability strategies in these nations replace the slash-and-burn strategies that are now so popular.

Cameroon provides an excellent example of this. One-third of this African nation's 475,000 square kilometers is covered with some of the world's oldest and densest rain forests. The rain forests of Cameroon have been classified by the World Bank as a "megadiversity" because they are home to a very high percentage of the Earth's species as well as several native tribes who have lived in a sustainable way with the rain forests for thousands of years. Politically, Cameroon is essentially a dictatorial police state, and the economic policies of the government are aimed at depleting these rain forests for cash (the rain forests are classified as national forests, and the government has bestowed upon itself the right to sell the resources). Even though the government's stated reason for doing this is to reduce the nations $4 billion foreign debt (a decision supported by most of Cameroon's international creditors), the debt has not decreased as a result of these policies; the only thing that has declined is the natural wealth of the nation and the homeland of many of its citizens (Horta, 1991). Most agree that changing the economic strategies practiced in Cameroon should begin with a change to a democratic form of government that respects the regional and cultural differences of the people. This should be followed by concerted efforts to find sustainable ways to employ the nation's incredible natural wealth. Obviously, these are tall orders, and accomplishing them will require tremendous outside efforts in addition to internal efforts. Organizations like the World Bank and the International Monetary Fund must provide support, as should the plethora of international business organizations (including creditors and logging companies) who have a stake in Cameroon's future.

We have devoted only a small amount of space to the issue of population control. However, the world's exponentially expanding population is certainly a major social barrier to achieving sustainability. Population growth is inversely related to economic wealth and education, and this has major implications for the global implementation of sustainability strategies. Population growth definitely represents a social barrier to implementing such strategies worldwide, but sustainability strategies are also a key to solving the Earth's population dilemma. If business strategies can be implemented in poor, Third World nations that would provide the people of these countries with opportunities to use their resources in sustainable ways as well as providing them with sufficient economic well-being, then population growth may be stymied. This is the major reason why sustainable economic systems are currently considered the most effective mechanisms for dealing with global social ills.

Changing Organizational Cultures

If sustainability strategies are to be successfully implemented in business organizations, it is necessary that the values for a small planet become the foundation of strategic decisions. This will require overcoming what is likely the most difficult of all barriers—changing organizational cultures. William Ruckelshaus (1991) makes it clear that the most significant ingredient in adopting sustainability as a value in business is bringing about change in the consciousness of people who manage and work in business organizations. He uses an excellent analogy to explain the magnitude of this problem. He points out that, whereas all organizations in capitalistic nations have a deep understanding and appreciation of the concept of profit, this concept had absolutely no meaning in the Soviet Union (a problem now causing serious difficulties in the newly independent republics' efforts to convert to free market economies). He believes that sustainability is as foreign a concept to strategic managers in capitalistic nations as profits are to managers in the former Soviet Republics. He says, "Sustainability has to be made the bones and belly of corporate life, to join the intrinsic concepts like profit and loss, debt and equity, capital and cost, that make our system work" (p. 7).

As we discussed in Chapter 4, the basic assumptions people make about the world determine the things they value, the things they pay attention to, and, ultimately, the things they do. In other words, human consciousness rests on the basic assumptions that people make about the world around them. Thus developing consciousness toward sustainability in business organizations means changing many of the basic assumptions on which businesses are founded.

Changing the basic assumptions of an organization is a very difficult task because those basic assumptions form the foundation for the organization's culture (Schein, 1985). And changing an organization's culture requires redefining what the organization stands for (its enterprise strategy); changing the nature of the work done by the organization; placing people in new roles that require new knowledge and new skills; and changing the objectives, performance measures, reward systems, training programs, and informal structures so that they support the new culture. Thus cultural change is a slow, evolutionary process that requires years, if it can be achieved at all.

Jim Post and Barbara Altman (1991) of Boston University provide some insight as to how formidable the cultural barriers are for implementing sustainability strategies in organizations. In their research of several firms, they conclude that long-term adoption of sustainability strategies will likely require a "third-order change" in the culture of organizations. First-order change (developing new ways to reinforce current objectives, values, norms, structures, etc.) and second-order change (purposefully modifying current objectives, values, norms, structures, etc.) are the normal focuses of a traditional organization's change efforts. However, third-order change is a different story; it requires that the organization adopt a completely new culture including new values, new objectives, new structures, and new norms. First-order and second-order changes are linear in nature, requiring that organizations do basically the same things they are currently doing, only better; however, third-order change is discontinuous change that requires the organization to achieve an entirely different qualitative state (Bartunek & Moch, 1987).

TQM-based sustainability strategies represent an example of how third-order change is probably necessary in order for firms to integrate the planet into their strategic processes. Jeffrey Heilpern and Terry Limpert (1991) of the Delta Consulting Group say that slow cultural change is a necessary part of adopting any TQM strategy in organizations. The basic problem they find when assisting firms in implementing TQM strategies is that the firms usually are founded on "quality-hostile" assumptions, such as assuming that profits are all that really matter or that the organization is a lot smarter than its customers. These assumptions are serious obstacles; before TQM can be implemented, firms must replace these "quality-hostile" assumptions with "quality-friendly" assumptions, such as defining quality by the customer and recognizing that profits result from high quality. Adding the sustainability dimension to TQM strategies presents an even more difficult cultural dilemma. Firms must adopt not only "quality-friendly" assumptions, but also "environment-friendly" assumptions, which form the basis of sustainability. Thus, if sustainability is as completely foreign a concept to strategic managers as Ruckelshaus (1991) contends, then changing organizational cultures to ones that incorporate TQM-based sustainability strategies will likely require a third-order change.

Thus a change in organizational cultures will ultimately prove to be the greatest barrier in organizational efforts to effectively implement sustainability strategies. Although this barrier poses some serious problems for organizations, it can be overcome. Business organizations have proven time after time that they can successfully adapt their cultures to new environmental conditions when necessary. As ecological concerns move closer and closer to the forefront of issues facing business, organizations that can adopt sustainability as the basis of their cultures will be prepared to develop ecologically-friendly market niches that allow them to thrive. Of course, organizations that cannot change their cultures in order to include sustainability will no doubt suffer, and some will not survive, but there is nothing really new about this. It has been known for a long time that no firm can survive unless it has a sufficient environmental niche in which to operate. As the environment changes, the niches change. Organizations will either find ways to adapt to these environmental challenges in a timely fashion or they will die.

Toward the Future

We would like to leave you with an image of the strategic manager of the future; one who guides a firm to economic success by serving the needs of the ultimate stakeholder: the Earth. Rather than simply describing such a strategic manager, we thought it would be better to provide an example of one, and we have chosen Ted Turner, Chairman of the Turner Broadcasting System (TBS). Egoism no doubt drives him (as it does most CEOs to some degree), and he could be criticized for this as easily as he can be praised for his environmental concerns. Nonetheless, he has succeeded in translating his long-term vision of a healthy, peaceful Earth into a corporation that has been economically successful while contributing to protecting the planet.

Our interest in Ted Turner's strategic management approach began when we heard him speak at the national convention of Women's Action for Nuclear Disarmament in Charlotte, North Carolina, in July, 1988. In the simple, direct, lazy-eyed style he is noted for, he said, "What good is it to make millions of dollars if we blow ourselves up?" For us, this statement summed up in 25 words or less why being concerned about protecting the environment is good business. His strong personal commitments to peace, social justice, and environmental protection are no secret; he espouses them in public on a regular basis. TBS sponsors the Goodwill Games, which are committed to promoting world peace, and Turner also started the Better World Society, which is founded on the principle that the power of the broadcast media can be an effective tool in achieving peace and environmental sustainability.

What makes him an excellent model of the future strategic manager, however, lies in the fact that he has been very effective in incorporating his social and ecological values into his business activities. He has diligently carved out an environmental and social niche for TBS in the broadcast media industry. Cable News Network (CNN) has strong environmental themes that run throughout its programming, and these themes are quite often related to business. For example, in June, 1991, CNN's two major business news shows, *Business Morning* and *Moneyline,* ran a 5-day series on the problems of safely disposing of high-level nuclear wastes. WTBS, the Atlanta-based superstation, also uses its airwaves to foster concerns about the environment. For example, in 1990 it introduced *Captain Planet* (developed by Turner himself), a cartoon show about an ecosystem hero who can only exist through combined international efforts; further, in 1991 it presented a 10-hour miniseries based on Michael Tobias's *Voice of the Planet.* These examples and the many hundreds of other hours of environmental programming on TBS networks exemplify strategic decisions that demonstrate a clear understanding that sustainability is the foundation on which business activities should be based in the future.

There are three basic points that we hope you have garnered from this book. First, the Earth has serious environmental problems that cannot be ignored, and many of these problems are directly related to the way humans think about and practice business. Second, responsible business in the 1990s and the 21st century should be conducted within the limits of the ecosystem; there is really no choice about this. Third, there are new, more realistic, ways of thinking about the relationship between business and the ecosystem, and these new ways of thinking are based on values that, when incorporated into the strategic management process, can be beneficial for both the long-run survival of the firm and the long-term survival of the Earth.

It is also important to recognize that this book only scratches the surface of a field in its infancy. It would be naive not to realize that there are many more questions than answers concerning what strategic managers need to know and to do in order to effectively merge sustainability into their decisions. Thus our hope is that managers and management scholars alike will begin the diligent search that is necessary if humankind is to find the elusive balance between the economic system and the ecosystem. The success of this search, we believe, rests on the willingness to include the greater ecosystem into business research and strategic decisions. The Earth is a small planet, and the Earth is the ultimate stakeholder in business organizations. Thus sustainability should become the basic foundation of strategic management in the years to come.

Note

1. The information on Ball Zinc Products Division and Great Dane Trailers of Tennessee came from the letters to the selection committee for the Governor's Award for Excellence in Hazardous Waste Management, which went on to present these firms the 1990 award.

References

Accelerated ozone loss cancer threat. (1991, April 5). *Johnson City Press*, p. 5.

The acid rain report. (1989, February). *Congressional Digest*, pp. 38-39.

Allen, F. E. (1991, April 17). McDonald's launches plan to cut waste. *The Wall Street Journal*, pp. B1, B6.

Ansoff, H. I. (1979). The changing shape of the strategic problem. In D. Schendel & C. Hofer (Eds.), *Strategic management: A new view of business policy and planning* (pp. 30-44). Boston: Little, Brown.

Argyris, C. (1957). *Personality and organization: The conflict between the system and the individual*. New York: Harper & Row.

Ayres, R. U. (1989). Industrial metabolism. In J. H. Ausubel & H. E. Sladovich (Eds.), *Technology and environment* (pp. 23-49). Washington, DC: National Academy Press.

Bader, G. (1986). The Scott Bader Commonwealth: Putting people first. *Long Range Planning, 19*(6), 56-74.

Bartunek, J. M., & Moch, M. K. (1987). First-order, second-order, and third-order change and organization development interventions: A cognitive approach. *Journal of Applied Behavioral Science, 23*, 483-500.

Begley, S., & Hager, M. (1991, June 10). Adam Smith turns green. *Newsweek*, p. 60.

Bell, T. D., Jr. (1990). Public initiatives: The power of the green consumer. In *Proceedings of the Business Week Symposium on The Environment: Corporate Stewardship and Business Opportunity in the Decade of Global Awakening* (pp. 19-21). New York: Journal Graphics.

Bemowski, K. (1991, April). Sorting fact from fiction. *Quality Progress*, pp. 21-25.

Benedick, R. E. (1990). Multilateral initiatives: The global policy push. In *Proceedings of the Business Week Symposium on The Environment: Corporate Stewardship and Business Opportunity in the Decade of Global Awakening* (pp. 11-13). New York: Journal Graphics.

Bennett, S. J. (1991). *Ecopreneuring: The complete guide to small business opportunities from the environmental revolution*. New York: Wiley.

Berry, T. (1988). *The dream of the Earth*. San Francisco: Sierra Club Books.

Blumenthal, K. (1989, November). Marketing with emotion: Wal-Mart shows the way. *The Wall Street Journal*, pp. B1, B4.

Boulding, K. (1970). Fun and games with the gross national product: The role of misleading indicators in social policy. In H. W. Helfrich (Ed.), *The environmental crisis* (pp. 157-170). New Haven, CT: Yale University Press.
Boulding, K. E. (1956). General systems theory: The skeleton of science. *Management Science, 2*(3), 197-208.
Boulding, K. E. (1966). The economics of the coming spaceship Earth. In H. Jarrett (Ed.), *Environmental quality in a growing economy* (pp. 3-14). Baltimore, MD: Johns-Hopkins Press.
Bremner, B. (1989, July 24). A new sales pitch: The environment. *Business Week,* p. 50.
Bridbord, K., Decoufle, P., & Fraumeni, J. (1978). *Estimates of the fraction of cancer in the United States related to occupational factors.* Bethesda, MD: National Cancer Institute, National Institute of Health Sciences, & Institute for Occupational Safety and Health.
Brown, W. Y. (1990). Shaping and entering international markets. In *Proceedings of the Business Week Symposium on The Environment: Corporate Stewardship and Business Opportunity in the Decade of Global Awakening* (pp. 57-59). New York: Journal Graphics.
Burns, T., & Stalker, G. M. (1961). *The management of innovation.* London: Tavistock Publications.
Buzzell, R. D., & Gale, B. T. (1987). *The PIMS principles.* New York: Free Press.
Campbell, J. (with Moyers, B.). (1988). *The power of myth.* New York: Doubleday.
Capra, F. (1975). *The tao of physics.* Boulder, CO: Shambhala Publications.
Capra, F. (1983). *The turning point.* New York: Bantam.
Carpenter, G. D. (1991). GEMI and the total quality journey to environmental excellence. *Proceedings of the First Conference on Corporate Quality/Environmental Management* (pp. 2-3). Washington, DC: Global Environmental Management Initiative.
Carroll, G. (1991, February/March). Green for sale. *National Wildlife,* pp. 24-27.
Cavanagh, G., Moberg, D., & Valasquez, M. (1981). The ethics of organizational politics. *Academy of Management Review, 6*(3), 363-374.
Chiras, D. D. (1991). *Environmental science: Action for a sustainable future.* Redwood City, CA: Benjamin/Cummings.
Christensen, C., Andrews, K., Bower, J., Hamermesh, R., & Porter, M. (1987). *Business policy: Text and cases* (6th ed.). Homewood, IL: Richard D. Irwin, Inc.
Clark, W. C. (1989, September). Managing planet Earth. *Scientific American,* pp. 47-54.
Coalition for Environmentally Responsible Economies. (1990). *The 1990 CERES guide to the Valdez Principles.* Boston: Author.
Cole, P., & Goldman, M. (1975). Occupations. In J. Fraumeni (Ed.), *Persons at high risk of cancer* (pp. 167-184). New York: Academic Press.
Commoner, B. (1990). *Making peace with the planet.* New York: Pantheon.
Corson, B., Marlin, A. T., Schorsch, J., Swaminathan, A., & Will, R. (1990). *Shopping for a better world.* New York: Council on Economic Priorities.
Council on Economic Priorities. (1991). *The better world investment guide.* Englewood Cliffs, NJ: Prentice-Hall.
Crosson, P. R., & Rosenberg, N. J. (1989, September). Strategies for agriculture. *Scientific American,* pp. 128-135.

Dadd, D. L., & Carothers, A. (1990, May/June). A bill of goods? Green consuming in perspective. *Greenpeace*, pp. 8-12.

Daly, H. E. (1977). *Steady state economics*. San Francisco: W. H. Freeman.

Daly, H. E. (1986). Toward a new economic model. *Bulletin of the Atomic Scientists, 42*(4), 42-44.

Daly, H. E., & Cobb, J. B., Jr. (1989). *For the common good*. Boston: Beacon.

Davis, G. R. (1990, September). Energy for planet Earth. *Scientific American*, pp. 55-62.

Deland, M. R. (1990). U.S. initiatives: Future policy directions. In *Proceedings of the Business Week Symposium on The Environment: Corporate Stewardship and Business Opportunity in the Decade of Global Awakening* (pp. 4-6). New York: Journal Graphics.

Denisi, A., Cafferty, T., & Meglino, B. (1984). A cognitive view of the performance appraisal process: A model and research proposition. *Organizational Behavior and Human Performance, 33*, 360-396.

Domini, A. L., & Kinder, P. D. (1986). *Ethical investing*. Reading, MA: Addison-Wesley.

Dougherty, E. (1990, April). Waste minimization: Reduce wastes and reap the benefits. *R & D Magazine*, pp. 62-67.

Dowd, A. R. (1991, May 20). The Democrats' desperate search. *Fortune*, pp. 119-120.

Drucker, P. (1980, Spring). Toward the next economics. *The Public Interest* [Special Issue: The Crisis in Economic Theory], pp. 4-18.

Drucker, P. (1989). *The new realities*. New York: Harper & Row.

Drucker, P. F. (1986). *The frontiers of management*. New York: E. P. Dutton.

Drucker, P. F. (1988, January/February). The coming of the new organization. *Harvard Business Review*, pp. 45-53.

Dumaine, B. (1990, May 7). Who needs a boss? *Fortune*, pp. 52-60.

Earth Works Group. (1989). *50 simple things you can do to save the Earth*. Berkeley, CA: Author.

Easterbrook, G. (1989, July 24). Cleaning up. *Newsweek*, pp. 26-29, 32-42.

Ehrlich, P. R., & Ehrlich, A. H. (1990). *The population explosion*. New York: Simon & Schuster.

Ehrlich, P. R., Ehrlich, A. H., & Holdren, J. P. (1977). *Ecoscience*. San Francisco: W. H. Freeman.

Eisenhart, T. (1990, November). McRecycle USA: Golden arches offers marketers a golden payoff. *Business Marketing*, pp. 25, 28.

Elkington, J., Hailes, J., & Makower, J. (1990). *The green consumer*. New York: Penguin.

Emery, F. E., & Trist, E. L. (1965). The causal texture of organizational environments. *Human Relations, 18*, 21-32.

Environmental Protection Agency, PBS Adult Learning Satellite Service, & Public Television Outreach Alliance. (1990, November 28). *Legal Winds of Change: Business and the New Clean Air Act* [Video conference]. Washington, DC: Authors.

Epstein, S. S. (1975). *The politics of cancer*. San Francisco: Sierra Club Books.

Ernst, K. R., & Baginski, R. M. (1989/1990). Visioning: The key to effective strategic planning. In H. E. Glass (Ed.), *Handbook of business strategy* (chap. 22). Boston: Warren, Gorham & Lamont.

Etzioni, A. (1988). *The moral dimension: Toward a new economics*. New York: Free Press.

Etzioni, A. (1991). What community, what responsiveness? *The Responsive Community,* 2(1), 5-8.

Faltermayer, E. R. (1989, July 17). Air: How clean is clean enough? *Fortune,* pp. 54-56, 58, 60.

Farnham, A. (1991, January 14). What comes after greed? *Fortune,* pp. 43-44.

Finney, M., & Mitroff, I. (1986). Strategic plan failures: The organization as its own worst enemy. In H. Sims & D. A. Gioia (Eds.), *The thinking organization* (pp. 317-335). San Francisco: Jossey-Bass.

Fisher, C., & Graham, J. (1989, August 21). Wal-Mart throws green gauntlet. *Advertising Age,* pp. 1, 66.

Flavin, C., & Lenssen, N. (1991, September/October). Here comes the sun. *World Watch,* pp. 10-18.

Freeman, R. E. (1984). *Strategic management: A stakeholder approach.* Boston: Pitman.

Freeman, R. E., & Gilbert, D. R., Jr. (1988). *Corporate strategy and the search for ethics.* Englewood Cliffs, NJ: Prentice-Hall.

French, H. F. (1990, November). *Green revolutions: Environmental reconstruction in eastern Europe and the Soviet Union* (Paper No. 99). Washington, DC: Worldwatch Institute.

Friedlander, S. K. (1989). Environmental issues: Implications for engineering design and education. In J. H. Ausubel & H. E. Sladovich (Eds.), *Technology and environment* (pp. 167-181). Washington, DC: National Academy Press.

Frierman, J. (1991, June 3). The big muddle in green marketing. *Fortune,* pp. 91-101.

Frosch, R. A., & Gallopoulos, N. E. (1989, September). Strategies for manufacturing. *Scientific American,* pp. 144-152.

Fulkerson, W., Judkins, R. R., & Sanghvi, M. K. (1990, September). Energy from fossil fuels. *Scientific American,* pp. 129-135.

Georgescu-Roegen, N. (1971). *The entropy law and the economic process.* Cambridge, MA: Harvard University Press.

Gibbons, J. H., Blair, P. D., & Gwin, H. L. (1989, September). Strategies for energy use. *Scientific American,* pp. 136-143.

Gibney, J. S. (1989, May 1). Washington diarist. *The New Republic,* p. 46.

Gillingham, P. N. (1979). The making of good work. In E. F. Schumacher (Ed.), *Good Work* (pp. 147-217). New York: Harper & Row.

Gioia, D. A. (1986). Conclusion: The state of the art in organizational social cognition. In H. Sims & D. A. Gioia (Eds.), *The thinking organization* (pp. 336-356). San Francisco: Jossey-Bass.

Gold, J. (1990, January 23). The pioneers. *Financial World,* pp. 56-58.

Goodpaster, K. E., & Matthews, J. B., Jr. (1982). Can a corporation have a conscience? *Harvard Business Review, 60*(1), 132-141.

Graedel, T. E., & Crutzen, P. J. (1989, September). The changing atmosphere. *Scientific American,* pp. 58-68.

Grammas, G. W. (1985). Quantitative tools for strategic decision making. In W. Guth (Ed.), *Handbook of business strategy* (chap. 15). Boston: Warren, Gorham, & Lamont.

Green Seal, Inc. (1990). Background on the Green Seal. Washington, DC: Author.

Greengard, S. (1990, November). Face values. *USAir Magazine,* pp. 88-97.

Growing greener. (1989, Fall). *Exchange,* pp. 1, 6-8.

Gutman, J. (1982). A means-end chain model based on consumer categorization processes. *Journal of Marketing, 46,* 60-72.

Halal, W. E. (1986). *The new capitalism.* New York: John Wiley & Sons.
Halal, W. E. (1990). The new management: Business and social institutions for the information age. *Business in the Contemporary World, 2*(2), 41-54.
Hambrick, D. C., & Brandon, G. L. (1987). Executive values. In D. C. Hambrick (Ed.), *The executive effect: Concepts and methods for studying top managers.* Greenwich, CT: JAI Press.
Hambrick, D., & Mason, P. (1984). Upper echelons: The organization as a reflection of its top managers. *Academy of Management Review, 9,* 193-206.
Handy, C. (1989). *The age of unreason.* Boston: Harvard Business School Press.
Hardin, G. (1968). The tragedy of the commons. *Science, 162,* 1243-1248.
Harman, W. W. (1990/1991, Winter). Review essay: *A cognitive theory of consciousness* by Bernard Baars. *Noetic Sciences Review,* pp. 38-40.
Hayes, D. (1990). Public initiatives: The power of the green consumer. In *Proceedings of the Business Week Symposium on The Environment: Corporate Stewardship and Business Opportunity in the Decade of Global Awakening* (pp. 16-19). New York: Journal Graphics.
Heilpern, J. D. (1990). Principles of total quality management [Summary]. *Proceedings of the of Total Quality Environmental Workshop* (pp. 5-7). Washington, DC: Global Environmental Management Initiative.
Heilpern, J. D., & Limpert, T. M. (1991). Building organizations for continuous improvement. *Proceedings of the First Conference on Corporate Quality/ Environmental Management* (pp. 11-15). Washington, DC: Global Environmental Management Initiative.
Heisenberg, W. (1985a). Science and the beautiful. In K. Wilber (Ed.), *Quantum questions* (pp. 55-68). Boston: New Science Library.
Heisenberg, W. (1985b). Scientific and religious truths. In K. Wilber (Ed.), *Quantum questions* (pp. 39-44). Boston: New Science Library.
Herman, R., Ardekani, S. A., & Ausubel, J. H. (1989). Dematerialization. In J. H. Ausubel & H. E. Sladovich (Eds.), *Technology and environment* (pp. 50-69). Washington, DC: National Academy Press.
Herzberg, F. (1960). *Work and the nature of man.* Cleveland, OH: World Publishing.
Hinrichsen, D. (1991, Spring). Economists' shining lie. *The Amicus Journal,* pp. 3-5.
Hoe, S. (1978). *The man who gave his company away.* London: William Heinemann.
Holdren, J. P. (1990). Energy in transition. *Scientific American,* pp. 157-163.
Hollender, J. A. (1990). *How to make the world a better place.* New York: Quill William Morrow.
Horta, K. (1991). The last big rush for the green gold. *The Ecologist, 21*(3), pp. 142-147.
Howard, J. A. (1977). *Consumer behavior: Application and theory.* New York: McGraw-Hill.
Howard, R. (1990, September/October). Values make the company: An interview with Robert Haas. *Harvard Business Review,* pp. 133-144.
Hull, R. (1990). European initiatives: Where is the EC heading? In *Proceedings of the Business Week Symposium on The Environment: Corporate Stewardship and Business Opportunity in the Decade of Global Awakening* (pp. 8-10). New York: Journal Graphics.
Hutterly, J. (1990). Public initiatives: The power of the green consumer. In *Proceedings of the Business Week Symposium on The Environment: Corporate*

Stewardship and Business Opportunity in the Decade of Global Awakening (pp. 22-23). New York: Journal Graphics.

Ilgen, D., & Feldman, J. (1983). Performance appraisal: A process focus. *Research in Organizational Behavior, 5,* 141-197.

Jolly, J., Reynolds, T., & Slocum, J. (1988). Application of the means-end theoretic for understanding the cognitive bases of performance appraisal. *Organizational Behavior and Human Decision Processes, 41,* 153-179.

Joseph, L. E. (1990). *Gaia: The growth of an idea.* New York: St. Martin's Press.

Kanter, D., & Mirvis, P. (1989). *The cynical Americans: Living and working in an age of discontent and disillusion.* San Francisco: Jossey-Bass.

Kelly, T. (1991, April). GEMI: The superhero of environmental management. *Quality Progress,* pp. 26-28.

Kirkpatrick, D. (1990, February 12). Environmentalism: The new crusade. *Fortune,* pp. 50-57.

Kleiner, A. (1991a, July/August). The three faces of Dow. *Garbage,* pp. 52-58.

Kleiner, A. (1991b, July/August). What does it mean to be green. *Harvard Business Review,* pp. 38-47.

Korzybski, A. (1933). *Science and sanity: An introduction to non-Aristotelian systems and general semantics.* Lakeville, CT: Institute of General Semantics.

Langone, J. (1989, January 2). A stinking mess. *Time,* pp. 44-47.

LeBlanc, C. (1991). *The nature of growth.* Washington, DC: National Audubon Society.

Lemonick, M. (1989, January 2). Feeling the heat. *Time,* pp. 36-39.

Levitt, T. (1987, November/December). The mixed metrics of greed. *Harvard Business Review,* pp. 6-7.

Lewin, K. (1947). Group decision and social change. In T. Newcomb & E. Hartley (Eds.), *Readings in social psychology* (pp. 330-344). New York: Henry Holt & Company.

Liedtka, J. M. (1989). Value congruence: The interplay of individual and organizational value systems. *Journal of Business Ethics, 8,* 805-815.

Likert, R. (1961). *New patterns of management.* New York: McGraw-Hill.

Linden, E. (1989, January 2). The death of birth. *Time,* pp. 32-35.

Lovelock, J. (1990). *The ages of Gaia.* New York: Bantam.

Lovins, A. B. (1989, February). *Energy, people and industrialization.* Paper presented to the Conference on Human Demography and Natural Resources, The Hoover Institution, Stanford University, Stanford, CA.

Lublin, J. S. (1991, March 5). Green executives find their mission isn't a natural part of corporate culture. *The Wall Street Journal,* pp. B1, B4.

Luthans, F., & Kreitner, R. (1985). *Organizational behavior modification and beyond: An operant and social learning approach.* Glenview, IL: Scott Forsman.

MacKenzie, J. C. (1991). Environmental leadership through quality. In *Proceedings of the First Conference on Corporate Quality/Environmental Management* (pp. 41-44). Washington, DC: Global Environmental Management Initiative.

MacKenzie, J. J., & ElAshry, M. T. (1989, April). Ill winds: Air pollution's toll on trees and crops. *Technology Review,* pp. 65-71.

Martz, L. (1990, May 21). Bonfire of the S&Ls. *Newsweek,* pp. 20-25.

Maurits la Riviere, J. W. (1989, September). Threats to the world's water. *Scientific American,* pp. 80-94.

Mazzocchi, T. (1990, July 7). *Economics and the work environment.* Paper presented at The Other Economic Summit, Houston, TX.

McCully, P. (1991). A message to the executives and shareholders of E. I. DuPont de Nemours and Imperial Chemical Industries, Ltd. *The Ecologist, 21*(3), 114-116.

McGregor, D. (1960). *The human side of enterprise.* New York: McGraw-Hill.

McMonies, D. (1985). The Scott Bader-Synthetic Resins saga. *Employee Relations, 7*(2), 20-25.

McNeill, J. (1989, September). Strategies for sustainable economic development. *Scientific American,* pp. 155-165.

McRobie, G. (1979). Preface. In E. F. Schumacher (Ed.), *Good Work* (pp. vii-xi). New York: Harper & Row.

Meznar, M. B., Chrisman, J. J., & Carroll, A. B. (1990, August). *Social responsibility and strategic management: Toward an enterprise strategy classification.* Paper presented at the meeting of the National Academy of Management, San Francisco, CA.

Milbrath, L. W. (1989). *Envisioning a sustainable society.* Albany: State University of New York Press.

Milbrath, L. W. (1990, July 7). *Redefining prosperity on the personal level.* Paper presented at The Other Economic Summit, Houston, TX.

Moberg, C. L., & Cohn, Z. A. (1991, May). Rene Jules Dubos. *Scientific American,* pp. 66-74.

Montaigne, Michel de (1958a). On the education of children. In J. M. Cohen (Trans.), *Michel de Montaigne essays* (pp. 60-65). Middlesex, UK: Penguin. (Original work published 1580)

Montaigne, Michel de (1958b). That one man's profit is another's loss. In J. H. Cohen (Trans.), *Michel de Montaigne essays* (pp. 48-53). Middlesex, UK: Penguin. (Original work published 1580)

Morgan, G. (1986). *Images of organizations.* Newbury Park, CA: Sage.

Nelson-Horchler, J. (1991, April 5). CEO pay: Baffling, disgraceful, sickening, embarrassing, infuriating. *Industry Week,* pp. 13-20.

Not in my back yard. (1991, March 4). *Time,* p. 53.

Nulty, P. (1990, August 13). Recycling has become big business. *Fortune,* pp. 81-86.

Odum, H. T. (1983). *Systems ecology.* New York: John Wiley & Sons.

Odum, H. T. (1990, July 7). *The prosperous way down.* Paper presented at The Other Economic Summit, Houston, TX.

Odum, H. T., & Odum, E. C. (1976). *Energy basis for man and nature.* New York: McGraw-Hill.

Ornstein, R., & Ehrlich, P. (1990). *New world, new mind.* New York: Touchstone.

Peto, R. (1985). The preventability of cancer. In M. Vessey & M. Gray (Eds.), *Cancer risk and prevention* (pp. 1-14). Oxford, UK: Oxford University Press.

Peters, T. (1990a, April 25). *Preparing Your Organization for the 21st Century* [Video conference]. Alexandria, VA: PBS, The Business Channel.

Peters, T. (1990b). Prometheus barely unbound. *Academy of Management Executive, 4*(4), 70-84.

Peters, T. J., & Waterman, R. H., Jr. (1982). *In search of excellence.* New York: Harper & Row.

Pinchot, G., III (1985). *Intrapreneuring.* New York: Harper & Row.

Pirsig, R. M. (1974). *Zen and the art of motorcycle maintenance: An inquiry into values.* New York: William Morrow.

Porter, M. E. (1985). *Competitive advantage.* New York: Free Press.

Porter, M. E. (1990). *The competitive advantage of nations.* New York: Free Press.

Porter, M. E. (1991, April). America's green strategies. *Scientific American*, p. 168.

Positive energy. (1991, March/April). *Sierra*, pp. 36-47.

Post, J. E. (1991, July/August). Managing as if the Earth mattered. *Business Horizons*, pp. 32-38.

Post, J. E., & Altman, B. (1991, August 12). *Corporate environmentalism: The challenge of organizational learning*. Paper presented at the meeting of the National Academy of Management, Miami, FL.

Postel, S. (1988, November/December). Global view of a tropical disaster. *American Forests*, pp. 25, 27-29, 69-71.

Postel, S. (1990, September/October). Toward a new "eco"-nomics. *World Watch*, pp. 20-28.

Rauber, P. (1990, July/August). The stockbroker's smile. *Sierra*, pp. 18-21.

Ravlin, E. C., & Meglino, B. M. (1987). Effect of values on perception and decision making: A study of alternative work values measures. *Journal of Applied Psychology, 72*(4), 666-673.

Research Alert. (1991). *Future vision.* Naperville, IL: Sourcebooks Trade.

Reynolds, T., & Jamieson, L. (1984). Image representations: An analytical framework. In J. Jacoby & J. Olson (Eds.), *Perceived qualities of products, services, and stores* (pp. 115-138). Lexington, MA: Lexington Books.

Rice, F. (1990, December 3). How to deal with tougher customers. *Fortune*, pp. 38-48.

Robertson, J. (1990). *Future wealth: A new economics for the 21st century.* New York: The Bootstrap Press.

Rock, S. (1989). Are greens good for you? *Director, 42*(6), 40-43.

Rokeach, M. J. (1968). *Beliefs, attitudes, and values.* San Francisco: Jossey-Bass.

Rosch, E., & Lloyd, B. (1978). *Cognition and categorization.* Hillsdale, NJ: Lawrence Erlbaum Associates.

Rose, F. (1990, October 8). A new age for business? *Fortune*, pp. 156-164.

Rose, R. A. (1990, September/October). Environmental investing. *Garbage*, pp. 50-53.

Rosenberg, M. (1956). Cognitive structure and attitudinal effect. *Journal of Abnormal and Social Psychology, 53*, 367-372.

Ross, M. H., & Steinmeyer, D. (1990, September). Energy for industry. *Scientific American*, pp. 89-98.

Ruckelshaus, W. D. (1991). Quality in the corporation: The key to sustainable development. *Proceedings of the First Conference on Corporate Quality/Environmental Management* (pp. 5-9). Washington, DC: Global Environmental Management Initiative.

Sale, K. (1985). *Dwellers in the land.* San Francisco: Sierra Club Books.

Sarney, G. (1990). Win-win strategies for business and environment in the world market. In *Proceedings of the Business Week Symposium on The Environment: Corporate Stewardship and Business Opportunity in the Decade of Global Awakening* (pp. 59-60). New York: Journal Graphics.

Satin, M. (1990, September 24). You don't have to be a baby to cry. *New Options*, pp. 1-4.

Schein, E. H. (1985). *Organizational culture and leadership.* San Francisco: Jossey-Bass.

Schneider, S. H. (1989, September). The changing climate. *Scientific American*, pp. 70-79.

Schorsch, J. (1990, April). It's not easy being green: Can our economy come clean? *Research Report.*

Schumacher, E. F. (1973). *Small is beautiful: Economics as if people mattered.* New York: Harper & Row.

Schumacher, E. F. (1977). *A guide for the perplexed.* New York: Harper & Row.

Schumacher, E. F. (1978). Foreword. In S. Hoe, *The man who gave his company away* (pp. xi-xiii). London: William Heinemann.

Schumacher, E. F. (1979). *Good work.* New York: Harper & Row.

Schwartz, J., Springen, K., & Hager, M. (1990, November). It's not easy to be green. *Newsweek,* pp. 51-52.

Schwenk, C. R. (1984). Cognitive simplification processes in strategic decision-making [sic]. *Strategic Management Journal, 5,* 111-128.

Schwenk, C. R. (1988). *The essence of strategic decision making.* Lexington, MA: Lexington Books.

Senge, P. M. (1990). *The fifth discipline: The art and practice of the learning organization.* New York: Doubleday/Currency.

Seventh Generation, Inc. (1991, Spring). *Seventh Generation catalog.* Colchester, VT: Author.

Shrivastava, P. (in press). CASTRATED environment: Greening organizational science. *Academy of Management Review.*

Slaba, S. M. (1990, May 18). When U.S. corporations go green—watch out. *The Christian Science Monitor,* p. 21.

Smith, R. B. (1990, April 16). Rush to endorse environmental goods sparks worry about shopper confusion. *The Wall Street Journal,* pp. B1, B4.

Speth, G. (1990). The crucial decade: Environmental imperatives for the 1990s. In *Proceedings of the Business Week Symposium on The Environment: Corporate Stewardship and Business Opportunity in the Decade of Global Awakening* (pp. 1-4). New York: Journal Graphics.

Spretnak, C., & Capra, F. (1986). *Green politics.* Santa Fe, NM: Bear & Company.

Stammer, L. B. (1989, March 6). Six more nations agree to sign ozone accord. *Los Angeles Times,* p. 1.

Stead, J. G., & Stead, W. E. (1986). Cancer prevention for the American worker: A never ending saga. *International Journal of Management, 3*(1), 41-49.

Stead, W. E., & Stead, J. G. (1980). Cancer in the workplace: A neglected problem. *Personnel Journal, 59*(10), 847-849.

Stead, W. E., Stead, J. G., & Worrell, D. L. (1990). An integrative model for understanding and managing ethical behavior in business organizations. *Journal of Business Ethics, 9,* 233-242.

Steiner, G., Miner, J., & Gray, E. (1986). *Management policy and strategy: Text, readings, and cases* (3rd ed). New York: MacMillan.

Stewart, T. A. (1991a, January 14). Should your company have a soul? *Fortune,* p. 33.

Stewart, T. A. (1991b, January 14). There are no products—only services. *Fortune,* p. 32.

Stipp, D. (1991a, February 28). Life-cycle analysis measures greenness, but results may not be black and white. *The Wall Street Journal,* p. B1.

Stipp, D. (1991b, March 14). Lunch-box staple runs afoul of activists. *The Wall Street Journal,* pp. B1, B8.

Stratton, B. (1991, April). Going beyond pollution control. *Quality Progress,* pp. 18-20.

Swanson, G. M. (1988). Cancer prevention in the workplace and natural environment: A review of etiology, research design, and methods of risk reduction. *Cancer, 62*(Suppl. 8), 1725-1746.

Thomas, R. (1991, May 6). Do CEOs make too much? *Newsweek,* p. 50.

Thomas, R., & Reibstein, L. (1991, June 17). The pay police. *Newsweek,* pp. 44-45.

Tobias, M. (1990). *Voice of the planet.* New York: Bantam.

Toufexis, A. (1989, January 2). Too many mouths. *Time,* pp. 48-50.

Turner, T. (1991, April). A tale of two birds: Courts move decisively to protect ancient forests [Special issue]. *In Brief,* p. 1-4.

Union of Concerned Scientists. (1990). *Cool energy: The renewable solution to global warming.* Boston: Author.

Van Gigch, J. P. (1978). *Applied general system theory.* New York: Harper & Row.

Vital signs. (1991, May/June). *World-Watch,* p. 6.

Wachtel, P. L. (1989). *The poverty of affluence.* Philadelphia, PA: New Society Publishers.

Walsh, J. P., & Ungson, G. R. (1991). Organizational memory. *Academy of Management Review, 16*(1), 57-91.

Weber, P. (1990, July/August). Green seals of approval heading to market. *World Watch,* pp. 7-8.

Weick, K., & Bougon, M. (1986). Organizations as cognitive maps. In H. Sims & D. A. Gioia (Eds.), *The thinking organization* (pp. 102-133). San Francisco: Jossey-Bass.

Weinberg, C. J., & Williams, R. H. (1990, September). Energy from the sun. *Scientific American,* pp. 147-155.

Weiner, J. (1990). *The next hundred years: Shaping the fate of our planet.* New York: Bantam.

White, D. (1989, November 26). Who ships toxic wastes? *The Birmingham News,* pp. 1A, 16A, 18A.

Whitehead, A. N. (1925). *Science and the modern world.* New York: Macmillan.

Wilber, K. (1985). *Quantum questions.* Boston: New Science Library.

Williams, R. M. (1960). *American society: A sociological interpretation* (2nd ed.). New York: Alfred A. Knopf.

Wilson, E. O. (1989, September). Threats to biodiversity. *Scientific American,* pp. 108-116.

Wood, B. (1984). *E. F. Schumacher: His life and thought.* New York: Harper & Row.

Woodruff, D., Peterson, T., & Lowery, K. (1991, April 8). The greening of Detroit. *Business Week,* pp. 54-60.

Woodward, J. (1965). *Industrial organization theory and practice.* Oxford, UK: Oxford University Press.

Worrell, D. L., & Gray, E. R. (1985). Uncle Remus meets regulatory reform: The brier-patch phenomenon. *Business Horizons, 28*(4), 63-67.

Yankelovich, D. (1981). *New rules.* New York: Random House.

Young, J. Y. (1991, May/June). Tossing the throwaway habit. *World Watch,* pp. 26-33.

Zenisek, T. J. (1979). Corporate social responsibility: A conceptualization based on organizational literature. *Academy of Management Review, 4*(2), 359-368.

Name Index

Subject Index

About the Authors

W. Edward Stead is Professor of Management at East Tennessee State University. He earned his PhD from Louisiana State University in 1976 and has been a faculty member at Western Illinois University, the University of Alabama in Birmingham, and Lousiana State University. He has published articles and cases on the moral implications of cost-benefit analysis, cancer in the workplace, ethical behavior in organizations, the social response process, green consumer values, group decision-making processes, and managing professionals. He has significant experience as a team building and management development consultant.

Jean Garner Stead earned her PhD from Louisiana State University in 1983, where she studied business and society under both Edmund Gray and Herman Daly. Her research on the moral implications of cost-benefit analysis, cancer in the workplace, ethical behavior in organizations, the social response process, and green consumer values has appeared in respected journals and books. She has served as a strategic management consultant for several large organizations. She is Associate Professor of Management at East Tennessee State University, where, in 1991, she received her third Outstanding Teacher Award in the College of Business.